GARDENER'S GUIDE TO
COMPACT PLANTS

JESSICA WALLISER

AUTHOR OF *CONTAINER GARDENING COMPLETE*

GARDENER'S GUIDE TO
COMPACT
PLANTS

EDIBLES & ORNAMENTALS FOR
SMALL-SPACE GARDENING

COOL
SPRINGS
PRESS

Brimming with creative inspiration, how-to projects, and useful information to enrich your everyday life, Quarto Knows is a favorite destination for those pursuing their interests and passions. Visit our site and dig deeper with our books into your area of interest: Quarto Creates, Quarto Cooks, Quarto Homes, Quarto Lives, Quarto Drives, Quarto Explores, Quarto Gifts, or Quarto Kids.

First Published in 2019 by Cool Springs Press,
an imprint of The Quarto Group,
100 Cummings Center, Suite 265-D,
Beverly, MA 01915, USA.
T (978) 282-9590 F (978) 283-2742
www.QuartoKnows.com

Cool Springs Press titles are also available at discount for retail, wholesale, promotional, and bulk purchase. For details, contact the Special Sales Manager by email at specialsales@quarto.com or by mail at The Quarto Group, Attn: Special Sales Manager, 100 Cummings Center, Suite 265-D, Beverly, MA 01915, USA.

23 22 21 20 19   1 2 3 4 5

ISBN: 978-0-7603-6484-0

Digital edition published in 2019

Library of Congress Cataloging-in-Publication Data available

Cover images: [Front] Holly Neel (illustration); Courtesy of Jessica Walliser, Vegetalis, Walter's Gardens, Garden Debut (l to r); [Back] Holly Neel (illustrations); Janet Loughrey with design by Helena Wagner, 4 Seasons Gardens, 4seasongardens.com
Design and Page Layout: James Kegley
Illustration: Holly Neel

Printed in China

For Mom and Dad—
thanks for always allowing
me to be curious about
the natural world
(and never getting mad
about the mess)

CONTENTS

INTRODUCTION

Gardening is a lot different today than it was a few generations ago. While our grandparents and great-grandparents focused on building victory gardens and feeding a houseful of children from an extensive backyard veggie patch, today's smaller families see gardening in a very different light. It's become a way to beautify our outdoor living spaces, satisfy our health-conscious appetites, and rejuvenate our work- and media-worn bodies and minds. Plants have become a symbol of calm in the hectic, digital lives of the millennial generation. Houseplants are having a renaissance, of sorts, and the presence of an incredible array of succulents on scores of windowsills, patios, and balconies is a sure sign that plants are still an important part of people's lives. The way people garden and their reasons for doing it, however, have definitely changed.

Not only have our gardening motivations evolved; so too have our gardens themselves. Today's gardens are vastly different from those of previous generations. While a 1/2-acre suburban lot with a modest house and a good-sized garden was the norm for many newly married baby boomers, today's young families are more likely to reside in big houses sandwiched onto ever-shrinking lots. Or, they live in urban environments where homes are close together, or in apartments, duplexes, townhomes, or condos with tiny yards or no yards at all. All this means that most modern gardeners have less room to grow. Couple that with our desire to nurture something beautiful and green (and our busy lives that are all too short on free time) and you have the perfect recipe for a new gardening niche—a niche that happens to be the very topic of this book: compact plants for small gardens.

Compact plants are those prized for their ability to start small and stay small, even when they reach full maturity. They're selected and bred by plant breeders for their petite form and well-behaved growth habit. With maintenance needs far less extensive than their full-sized counterparts, compact plants are the perfect fit for anyone looking to create a beautiful small-scale garden and reduce the amount of time needed to maintain their landscape. These plants are also an ideal choice for container gardeners, since most require less room for both their top growth and their root system.

Compact edibles are ideal for small kitchen gardens, raised beds, and containers. They allow you to grow plenty of homegrown produce without taking up a lot of real estate.

There are dozens of varieties of compact trees, shrubs, and perennials, many of which you'll meet in chapter 5. They offer the same gorgeous blooms, lush foliage, and seasonal interest as their full-sized cousins but in a far smaller package. And just like their larger kin, many of these compact ornamental plants also help sustain backyard wildlife—such as birds, butterflies, and bees—via their flowers, berries, and foliage.

There are also plenty of compact edible plants, including dwarf berries, vegetables, fruit trees, and herbs, that are an excellent choice for gardeners who want to feed their families fresh, organic produce without requiring an extensive backyard or blowing their grocery budget. Chapter 6 is dedicated to this group of fantastic and productive plants. You'll find detailed profiles of fifty different small-statured edibles ideal for a petite kitchen garden, a collection of containers, or a small raised bed.

Compact plants also play an important role in addressing problematic areas in the landscape. Chapter 4 outlines eight common landscape problems and offers you a list of multiple compact plants capable of combating each particular problem. Whether you're looking to screen out a nosy neighbor, cover a steep slope, bring a splash of color to a shady site, or spruce up a drab winter garden, this chapter on compact plants with purpose has you covered.

In addition to these three chapters filled to the brim with profiles of unique small-scale plants that are sure to become new favorites, you'll also learn where these minivarieties come from, how to shop for them, and even how to plant each type. And no book on gardening with compact plants would be complete without a well-formulated list of suggested maintenance tips for keeping your plants in prime condition from the start of the growing season to the finish. Though compact plants generally have reduced maintenance needs when compared to many other types of plants, chapter 2 covers the ins and outs of watering, fertilizing, and mulching these small specimens, as well as the importance of deadheading, pinching, and occasionally pruning.

> "With maintenance needs far less extensive than their full-sized counterparts, compact plants are the perfect fit for anyone looking to create a beautiful small-scale garden and reduce the amount of time needed to maintain their landscape."

But the most creative aspects of gardening with compact plants are addressed in chapter 3, where you'll discover a plethora of practical design tips, plus ten inspiring landscape designs using only compact plants. I've brought in the experts for this chapter, asking ten different gardening professionals to formulate ten different ready-made plans you can use to quickly build a beautiful, professionally designed, small-scale garden of your own. From a front-entrance planting with compact evergreens and a shady nook filled with low-growing perennials to a pint-sized pollinator garden and a tiny backyard plot overflowing with micro-vegetables, these design plans are sure to give you a leg up on creating a gorgeous garden in even the tightest quarters.

And last, on page 196 of this book, you'll find a source list, filled with the names and contact information for dozens of nurseries, wholesalers, and online retailers who sell the plants featured in the previous pages. These are the breeders, growers, and champions of the small-plant movement. Support them and they'll continue to provide an even greater variety of compact plants for a new generation of gardens.

My hope is that the *Gardener's Guide to Compact Plants* becomes a much-loved copilot on your journey toward building the lush and productive small-scale garden of your dreams. Once you see the breathtaking diversity of plants available to fill your garden with food and beauty, you'll realize the possibilities truly are endless.

1

IT'S A SMALL-PLANT WORLD
What Are Compact Plants and Where to Find Them

Before introducing you to some of the best small-plant varieties for your landscape and discussing how to plant and care for them, it's important to understand what makes a particular plant fit into the category of "compact." What traits must it have to be considered small when compared to its relatives? And where do these plants come from in the first place?

WHAT EXACTLY IS A COMPACT PLANT?

As with people, plants come in a wide array of shapes and sizes. While some landscapes are large enough to handle a tree that grows 60 feet tall or a shrub that spreads 12 feet wide, lots of backyards don't have enough space for such a substantial specimen. Not to mention the fact that many homeowners aren't interested or able to be constantly pruning their plants to make them fit into a smaller yard. Thankfully, the nursery industry has taken notice of all of this, and it continues to develop and select plants with a restricted size for these smaller yards and gardens (more on this process in a bit).

Exactly which plants can be called compact is certainly debatable, but basically, when a particular plant variety exhibits a substantially reduced size when compared to other normal plants of the same species, that particular variety can be considered compact (sometimes also called dwarf). This size reduction can be exhibited in either the plant's height or width—or, often, both. While the limited stature of these plants doesn't necessarily make them miniatures (which is a whole other category of plants), it does indicate that the plants have a growth habit that's smaller than normal for their species. In some cases, the speed of growth is limited, too.

There are hundreds of compact tree, shrub, and perennial varieties, many of which are featured throughout this book. Let's take a closer look at each of these three groups separately and determine which traits they might have that make them "compact."

Trees

NARROW GROWTH: When a tree is thinner than other trees within that same species, its slender form makes that variety fit under the umbrella of compact plants. Narrow trees that have a single trunk are called **columnar trees**. They may have upright branches or drooping pendulous ones, but their branches are always shorter and held close to the trunk. **Fastigiate trees**, on the other hand, are another group of tall, narrow trees; but these trees have multiple trunks or longer branches that reach straight up to the sky to create the narrow form. Both, though, are considered compact plants, even though some varieties of columnar and fastigiate trees can grow 60 feet tall or more. There are plenty of both types of these trees, however, that aren't nearly as tall.

In chapters 4 and 5, I detail several varieties of these trees that are beautiful landscape plants, but a great example is the Apollo® Sugar Maple (*Acer saccharum* 'Barrett Cole'). While standard sugar maples have a massive canopy spread that can quickly overtake even a modestly large backyard, Apollo® maxes out at just 8 to 10 feet wide, about a quarter of the size of a typical sugar maple. (You'll find more about this variety in chapter 5.) Columnar and fastigiate trees are excellent for tight quarters, between homes, along streets, and next to patios—anywhere where wide branches wouldn't be suitable.

Slender trees, such as this 'Wissel's Saguaro' false cypress, also fall under the umbrella of compact plants. While they're tall, they don't take up much room in the landscape.

SHORT STATURE: Trees can also be considered compact if their mature height is substantially shorter than others within their species. More often than not, this reduced height is coupled with a reduced spread as well, making these trees choice selections for postage stamp–sized yards or petite planting beds. Typically, compact trees in this category grow to less than half of the height of their relatives. A good example is the Sargent Tina Crabapple. This compact variety of the standard crabapple has beautiful blooms and is incredibly hardy, and it tops out at just 5 feet tall and 6 feet wide (see chapter 5 for more on the Sargent Tina Crabapple).

Shrubs

When it comes to shrubs, the compact trait is most often shown in both the height and width of the mature plant. This means these shrubs keep their small stature without a lot of pruning or fuss. There are two basic groups of compact shrubs to be on the lookout for.

DECIDUOUS FLOWERING SHRUBS: These compact shrubs may have a reduced size, but they almost always produce full-sized blooms. Though they lose their leaves in the winter, shrubs in this group are real knockouts in the landscape. They have all the bloom power of their standard-sized cousins but in an itty-bitty package.

Compact shrubs that produce edible berries, such as this blueberry, keep their small stature and require little to no pruning.

EVERGREEN SHRUBS: Though there are plenty of deciduous flowering shrubs for homeowners to include in their gardens, there are scores of compact evergreen shrubs, too. While some are needled evergreens, others are broad-leaved evergreens that may or may not produce showy blooms (think rhododendrons, azaleas, and laurels). But regardless of whether they're needled or broad-leaved, evergreen varieties are terrific for foundation plantings, shrub islands, mixed borders, and even low hedgerows where the homeowner wants something "green" all year round.

You'll find specifics on a wide selection of both deciduous and evergreen compact shrub varieties in chapters 4 and 5.

Perennials

Compact perennials are the ideal fit for the front of foundation plantings, along sidewalks, next to patios and decks, in flower beds and borders, around mailboxes, and even in containers. The blooms of these plants are standard size for their species; it's just the plant's foliage height that's smaller. Overall, dwarf perennials are lower growing, reaching a far shorter height than normal varieties of the same species. However, with a few exceptions, most spread just as wide as their full-sized counterparts, though they may take their time getting there.

Perennials are herbaceous plants that do not produce woody growth and return to the garden year after year, springing out of the ground when spring arrives as long as they're planted in a region where they'll survive the winter. Like trees and shrubs, perennials are classified in part by the hardiness zones in which they will survive.

In each of the plant profiles in subsequent chapters of this book, you'll find I've noted the lowest winter temperature down to which each plant variety will survive without damage. This can help you determine which varieties of compact trees, shrubs, and perennials will grow in your garden.

Compact perennials can be used in flower beds and borders, at the front of homes, along sidewalks, and in many other areas. Here, they add color to a shady container in the corner of a small patio.

WHERE DO SMALL-STATURED PLANTS COME FROM?

Now that you know what traits make a plant compact, it's time to discover where these plants come from. Despite what certain scare-tactic "news" articles may lead you to believe, the compact plants available to homeowners are not the result of some funky genetic-engineering technique. Yes, there are some dwarf farm crops that were created through genetic engineering, but as of this writing, there are no genetically engineered ornamental plants on the market. Instead, compact plants are selected or developed in one of three different ways.

First, compact plants can be selectively bred through classic plant-breeding methods where the breeder selects for the desired trait of a reduced mature plant size. Breeders look at a group of plants and select the most compact ones of the bunch; then they cross those plants with other shorter-statured selections. Eventually, through numerous judicious crosses over several generations, the dwarfing trait becomes more pronounced and stable. This method has been

Trial gardens, like this one, grow and test many different varieties, carefully selecting only the best ones to bring to market.

used by farmers and plant breeders since the dawn of agriculture to breed for any number of different desired traits, including things like bloom size, color, or time; improved hardiness or yields; disease resistance; or any other positive attributes that may be deemed desirable. This is a common method for creating compact vegetables, annuals, and perennial plant varieties. It's less common, however, with trees and shrubs because it requires a far longer span of time for these types of plants to reach maturity.

Next, compact plants can be chosen from natural genetic variants found in a population of the plants. Genetic mutations occur frequently in the plant world, especially when growing from seed; and often, when examining a large group of seedlings, one can see a few natural genetic variations within the group. Whether it's a random leaf variegation, a different flower color, or a change in plant stature or structure, genetic mutations happen often. Horticulture professionals, growers, and plant breeders are always on the prowl for natural variants that show desired traits. So, for example, if one seedling in a group of 100 grew to half the height of the others, it may be selected and grown to maturity to see if that dwarfing trait is also exhibited in the full-grown plant. If it is, the breeder may then decide to propagate the plant vegetatively to ensure the trait is present in future generations (more on this in a moment).

Natural genetic variants are sometimes found in nature, as well. Many of the compact trees and shrubs featured in this book were originally discovered as a single random specimen at a botanic garden, a breeding facility, a nursery, a private garden, or even in the wild. In most of these cases, the plants are then propagated vegetatively. Since these types of compact plants seldom grow true from seed (meaning plants grown from seeds harvested from these plants will not carry the same dwarfing trait), they are instead grown via leaf, stem, or root cuttings taken from the single "mother plant" that showed the desired genetic variation. Vegetative propagation can also take place via a tissue culture lab, or in the case of herbaceous perennials, vegetative propagation may occur through crown division. When plants are vegetatively propagated in any one of these ways, they are an exact clone of the "mother plant" they came from, which means, of course, that the compact trait is definitely present in all future generations.

Third, plants can be made to stay compact via a process called grafting. Grafting is a centuries-old craft in which a person takes pieces from two or more different plants and grafts them together so they grow as one plant. The grafting process is performed because it brings multiple positive traits from separate plants into a single plant. It's a technique that can be used to create plants with improved disease resistance and hardiness, increased yields, or unique physical forms, such as topiaries, standards, weeping branches, and yes, compact growth habits.

Though there are many different types of grafting, in its simplest form, grafting attaches the shoot system (the scion) of one plant to the root system (the rootstock) of a separate plant. The two are grafted together in a fairly simple procedure, and once the graft union has healed, the two plants grow as one. In most cases, the scion and rootstock must be from the same species (or, sometimes, the same family) in order for them to be compatible with each other and for the graft union be successful. In other words, you can't graft a juniper with an oak tree. But, you can graft an apricot with a peach tree because they're in the same stone-fruit family.

« Many compact trees, shrubs, and perennials are propagated by stem cuttings so the traits controlling their height are also found in the offspring. Vegetative cuttings such as these are an exact clone of the parent plant.

Nursery professionals sometimes use grafting to create dwarf or compact plants by selecting and using a specific rootstock with dwarfing traits. Then, they graft the shoot system of a full-sized compatible variety of that plant on top of the rootstock. The dwarfing trait in the rootstock is then transferred to the shoot system, yielding dwarf fruit trees, some types of dwarf evergreens, or other compact plants.

Grafting is quite common among fruit and ornamental trees, especially those with unique or specialized forms. For example, many weeping trees are created by grafting a pendulous shoot system onto a straight-trunked variety of the same plant, and some Japanese maples and fruit trees may be grafted onto different rootstocks in order to improve their winter hardiness. Novelty pom pom bushes are often created through grafting, as well.

One slightly newer way the technique of grafting has found its way into our gardens is through vegetables. Some seed and plant catalogs are now carrying grafted tomatoes, peppers, melons, and other vegetables. Grafted vegetables are created by selecting a great-tasting, heavy-yielding variety and grafting it to a rootstock with improved disease and pest resistance, early maturity, drought tolerance, and/or vigorous growth. The idea is that these grafted plants will perform better and produce

Dwarf fruit trees, such as this container-grown pear tree, are created through the process of grafting.

earlier than those vegetables that are ungrafted. As of this writing, to my knowledge there are no dwarf vegetables that are created through grafting; but I have no doubt they are a part of gardening's future.

Keep in mind, though, that grafting is useful only for the generation of plants on which it was performed. The improvements or dwarfing traits made through grafting are not carried to the next generation via saved seeds or even by taking cuttings of the plant. It's just for a single generation.

THE BIG FAKE-OUT

There is another method that greenhouses and commercial growers sometimes use to keep plants more compact and tidy, but it's one that's both temporary and, some say, questionable. Plant-growth regulators (PGRs) are chemical sprays that influence various plant hormones and cause an artificial and temporary mutation in the plant they're applied to. Several different PGRs are used for a number of different reasons, but the ones I want to focus on here are applied to plants to inhibit their growth and keep the plants' stems shorter.

Proponents say that using PGRs makes plants more attractive to the consumer (read: more neat and tidy) and easier to handle in the greenhouse (it's tough to transport or sell a flat full of tall, leggy plants all tangled together). Those against using PGRs for height control in plant production note that few studies have been done to examine the safety of these chemicals, especially when used on edible plants like vegetables and herbs, or on the amount of residual PGRs remaining in these plants at the time of consumption.

Whether you're pro or con when it comes to PGRs, it's important to understand that once these plants are moved out into the landscape and applications are stopped, the plant will eventually revert to its normal size and growth habit. Don't be fooled by PGRs. Do your homework and make sure the plant you're purchasing hasn't been forced into dwarfism via these products, only to grow back into a full-sized plant when placed in your garden.

THE COMPANIES THAT SELECT, GROW, AND SELL COMPACT PLANTS

Several decades ago, when I first entered the nursery trade, you had to go to your local family-run nursery to purchase plants. The nursery staff who worked there probably started most of their annual, perennial, and vegetable plants from seeds, divisions, or cuttings. They may have had field rows full of trees and shrubs out back, behind the greenhouse, from which they propagated and dug their nursery stock each spring. Yes, some garden centers purchased trees, shrubs, houseplants, and poinsettia cuttings from other nurseries; but they almost always played a huge hand in growing the plants they sold.

Now, things are a bit different in the nursery industry. Many (but not all) independent greenhouses and garden centers don't actually grow much of their plant stock from scratch.

Very few nursery managers still grow all of their own stock from seed or cuttings. Most now purchase their plant stock from larger outside growers and propagators.

Instead, they purchase immature plants from a larger commercial grower or a company that specializes in propagation, and then they pot those small plants into bigger containers in-house and grow them out to a salable size. Or, they buy and then resell already-mature plant material to their customers, having it shipped in from a diversity of wholesalers. Very few independent nurseries grow 100 percent of the nursery stock they sell at their operations anymore. In many ways, it's a system that's far more economical for these small businesses and a lot less labor intensive.

An improved distribution network allows many nurseries to get new plants in stock fairly quickly, though they tend to carry fewer varieties than in decades past.

There are plenty of pros and cons to both the old and new way the nursery industry operates, however. Unfortunately, many smaller independent nurseries have closed down in recent years due to a variety of factors. The increased availability of cheaply priced plants at big-box retailers who purchase their plants in massive quantities from a network of contract growers is certainly one of those factors. But, as most gardeners come to realize, cheap doesn't necessarily equal better. Independent nurseries care for their plants properly from start to sale, which, from my experience, can't always be said about the staff at big-box stores.

Another perceived negative of this modern system is that some independent garden centers are limited in the variety of plants they have for sale. Plants can now be patented, preventing nursery owners from taking cuttings of these patented varieties and starting more plants on their own. And, if they're buying their starter stock from another grower, nursery owners are limited to whatever varieties are grown there.

A positive of this new nursery industry, however, is definitely increased plant availability, especially of a broad diversity of nationally branded plants. Years ago, it was often very difficult to find a specific plant, particularly if it was something a bit more unusual. You were limited to whatever your local nursery happened to grow that year. Now, even if a garden center doesn't have a specific plant in stock, most can go to their broker network and get that plant for you in a fairly short amount of time. The distribution network and availability of plant material is, in many ways, much improved. If you read about a cool plant in a newspaper article (or this book!), chances are that you can readily get that plant either from one or more nurseries fairly close to home or from any number of mail-order nurseries who will ship it right to your door.

This modern nursery system is probably more pro than con to those seeking out compact plants. Plant breeders and growers develop, select, grow, and sell small-statured varieties to garden centers and direct to consumers more than ever before. Compact plants are among the most desired goals of the industry because there is a rapidly expanding need for them in the marketplace. It appears that the small-plant trend is here to stay. People want no-fuss plants that don't require pruning and fit nicely into their smaller, modern yards and gardens.

As mentioned in the book's introduction, at the back of this book you'll find a source list. In it you'll find many companies who breed, grow, and market the compact plant varieties found within these pages. If you find a plant in this book that you want to grow (I hope there are many), you'll find that plant via one or more of the companies in the source list.

WHAT TO LOOK FOR WHEN SHOPPING FOR COMPACT PLANTS

Beyond the specific varieties of compact plants introduced later in this book, there are many others to be discovered. But how do you know a plant is going to be compact when you spy its colorful blooms or beautiful foliage on a trip to the garden center? Thankfully, there are many different clues to look for to help determine whether or not a plant has a more compact form.

IF YOU'RE SHOPPING AT A NURSERY, THESE FOUR ARE A GOOD START:

1. THE TEXT ON THE PLANT'S POT TAG. There's language to be on the lookout for when reading a plant's pot tag. Phrases like "compact form," "bush-type," "container-friendly," "small-statured," "low-growing," and the like will be on the tags of varieties that are compact or dwarf in form. Read the nursery's signage and any materials displayed with the plants themselves for clues on the plant's growth habit. The mature height and width of the plant are almost always clearly noted on the pot tag.

2. THE BOTANICAL NAME OF THE PLANT. Botanical names themselves have much to offer in terms of what they can tell you about a plant. Botanical names are binomial. The first word is the name of the genus of that plant, and the second is the specific epithet (commonly called the species). Sometimes, there's an additional name after those two, in a set of single quotation marks. This is the cultivar (or variety) name of that species of plant. The cultivar name itself may indicate a compact growth habit (e.g., 'Walker's Low' catmint, 'Tiny Tim' tomato, and 'Dwarf Pagoda' Japanese holly), but the Latin botanical name sheds even more light on specific plant traits. Keep a sharp eye out for species names that indicate some form of compact growth habit, including *nana*, *compacta*, *alpinus*, *prostrata*, *procumbens*, *minima*, *minor*, *columnar*, and *fastigiate*, to name just a few.

3. ASK SOMEONE. It may seem like a no-brainer to ask for help when you need it, but sometimes we all need to be reminded that there's no shame in asking for help. If you do your plant shopping at an independent, local garden center, there should always be someone there who's willing to answer any and all questions you have about the growth habits of any plant. And if they don't know the answer off the top of their head, hopefully they can refer you to another employee or a reference book they keep close at hand.

4. USE YOUR CELL PHONE. If you have questions no one can answer, don't be afraid to use Google. But, as I'm sure you already know, you can't believe everything you read on the internet. Rely only on the information available from university extension service websites or those written by industry professionals, nursery operators, professional growers, horticulturists, professors, and others who work the trade. Do not rely on information posted by well-meaning bystanders in the comment section of somebody's Facebook post. If you want accurate, university-distributed information about plants, simply add "site:edu" to the end of whatever phrase or word you're Googling. For example, if you're looking for a few good urban street trees, type "urban street trees site:edu" into the search bar. The first hits will be links to the topic only on university websites. It's a lifesaver for anyone who wants to avoid bad information on the internet.

IF YOU'RE SHOPPING FROM A SEED CATALOG OR ONLINE SOURCE FOR COMPACT VEGETABLES, THERE ARE TWO ADDITIONAL THINGS TO WATCH FOR:

1. LOOK FOR KEYWORDS. When seeking out compact vegetable varieties in a catalog, look for words and phrases like "bush-type," "compact," "container-friendly," and "small-statured." They all translate to a smaller-than-normal growth habit for that particular vegetable.

2. CHECK THE DISEASE-RESISTANCE KEY CODE. While it has nothing to do with whether or not a plant is compact, most seed companies have a disease resistance key somewhere in their catalog or on their website that's well worth paying attention to. In the description of each different vegetable variety, and often on the seed packet itself, there are code letters that note which pathogens that particular variety is resistant to (i.e., PM = powdery mildew, BW = bacterial wilt or TMV = tobacco mosaic virus). When shopping for compact vegetable varieties, you should also pay attention to this code and try to select cultivars with a natural resistance to common diseases. It saves you a lot of trouble later in the season.

Dwarf tomatoes, like this one, are a great fit for containers. When seeking compact varieties, look for terms such as "compact form," "bush type," or "container-friendly" for clues about the plant's mature height.

A WORD ON COMPACT PLANTS AND POLLINATORS

Before wrapping up this chapter and moving on to tips for planting and maintaining compact plants, it's worth taking a brief look into a topic that's of great concern to many gardeners: the health of our pollinators.

As you may already know, European honeybees aren't the only important pollinators to make a home in our yards and gardens. In fact, North America is home to some 4,000 species of native bees—from fat and sassy bumblebees to tiny, iridescent sweat bees—many of which are facing population declines due to habitat loss, lack of forage, and pesticide exposure.

There's been much talk in the gardening world about how plant breeding and the introduction of various cultivars of plants impact the health of pollinators. On the tip of many a tongue, my own included, are questions like

- When a plant is bred to have bigger blooms, how does that impact the accessibility of its nectar?

- Can pollinators access pollen and nectar from the thick layers of petals when we breed a plant to produce double flowers?

- When we change the color of a flower through breeding, does that impact a pollinator's ability to find that plant?

- Does breeding for a shorter or taller plant stature impact nectar accessibility to certain low- or high-flying insects?

- When we breed a plant to appeal only to a human's sense of beauty, how does that impact the quality and quantity of the nectar it produces?

As the author of *Attracting Beneficial Bugs to Your Garden*, I have a keen interest in understanding the role our plant choices have in supporting our native insects. It's led me to carefully consider each plant I think about adding to my own garden before bringing it home and planting it.

Many compact plants, such as this Sapphire Surf™ bluebeard (*Caryopteris* x *clandonensis* 'Blauer Splatz'), attract and support pollinators, though it's important to consider many factors when determining the pollinator appeal of a particular plant.

A few studies have been done, with more under way, that examine the pollinator appeal of plant cultivars and the effects of plant breeding on nectar quality and fitness. Some folks think the impact of this breeding on pollinating insects is minimal, as evidenced by the number and diversity of insects foraging on the plants' nectar, while others sing the praises of using only regionally native plants that have not been bred into cultivar form. Both sides are passionate and vocal. Do I have the answer? No, certainly not. But I do know that in my own garden, I have a mixture of native plants in their straight species form, along with lots of cultivars of both native and non-native plants. My personal belief is that creating a pesticide-free habitat, full of a broad diversity of plants, flower structures and colors, and bloom times is key to supporting all types of insects, including pollinators.

As you'll soon see, there are many compact plant varieties that are known to support a diversity of pollinators in the landscape, and including them in your garden doesn't just add beauty; it also adds forage and habitat for these insects.

WHAT'S NEXT?

Now that you know a bit more about the traits that make a plant compact, how these plants are brought to market, and what to look for on your next shopping trip, it's time to look at how best to plant and care for them.

There are over 4000 species of native bees, including this tiny sweat bee, that use our yards and gardens as a source of nutrition and habitat. »

SELECTING, PLANTING, AND MAINTAINING COMPACT PLANTS

Walking into a garden center filled to the brim with plants may seem a little intimidating, especially for those new to gardening. But, if you take some time to ask yourself a few questions before you walk in the door, you'll be better prepared for a successful shopping trip.

SELECTING THE BEST COMPACT PLANTS FOR YOUR GARDEN

There are many things to consider when deciding which compact plants to include in your landscape. Here's a simple step-by-step process to follow, whether you're planting a whole new garden area or adding new plants to an existing one.

STEP 1: START BY THINKING ABOUT THE SPECIFICS OF THE GARDEN AREA YOU WANT TO PLANT IN. Site conditions and purpose dictate plant choices in a big way. If your objective is to spruce up the foundation plantings around your house, you'll be using different compact plants than you would use if you were putting in your first vegetable garden. This step involves looking at not just the area itself but also its purpose. Are you planting an edible garden, one that appeals to pollinators, a border for a children's play area, or a patio planting that's especially appealing at night?

Also jot down notes about the physical conditions of the site—things like how much sun the area receives throughout the day and whether the soil there is waterlogged, gritty and dry, or somewhere in between. Use these pieces of information to inform your decisions and make sure that each plant you choose is suitable to both the site's growing conditions and its purpose.

STEP 2: WHAT'S YOUR GOAL? Next, you'll want to take a hard look at what goal you're trying to achieve with the planting and match that goal with a specific group of plants. Take notes about how the space is to be used and what you're hoping to accomplish by planting there. For example, if your goal is to add a pop of color down your front walk, you should walk right past the compact evergreens and head straight to the compact perennials. If you want to create a defined border between your house and your neighbor's, low-growing herbs shouldn't be your first choice. Instead, opt for columnar trees, narrow ornamental grasses, or a low hedge of compact evergreen shrubs.

When selecting compact plants for your garden, it's important to consider what the space will be used for and what the growing conditions are.

There are lots of factors to take into consideration, such as whether you want a plant that flowers or a nonflowering specimen. Or, are you hoping to harvest something edible or do you just want pretty flowers? Is a low-maintenance landscape your goal? Then maybe perennials that need to be sheared back three times a season aren't the best choice. Write down your goals for that area and which groups of plants you think best accomplish it.

Chapter 4, "Compact Plants with Purpose," is aimed at simplifying this step by providing you with lists of specific compact plant varieties that accomplish particular goals, making your trip to the garden center a whole lot easier. It's particularly useful if you have a challenge to overcome, beyond just wanting to beautify your outdoor living space. There are plant lists for eight different purposes, from covering sloped sites to adding winter interest.

STEP 3: CHOOSE PLANTS TO MEET YOUR GOALS. The third and final step in the process also tends to be the most overwhelming. Paring down your choices to ensure that each and every one of them is a perfect match to the site, its purpose, and your goals, all while considering how they'll look when paired together, is a complicated task. Some gardeners love this step, adding new plants to their garden on a regular basis, while others struggle to make their decisions, perhaps fearing they'll make a bad choice and waste time and money.

If you're intimidated by the thought of having to hand-select every plant and decide what to plant where, chapter 3, "Designing with Compact Plants," will come in handy. In it are ten professionally designed landscape plans featuring compact plants in small spaces. Use these plans and plant lists in your own yard to simplify the process and create a garden space that meets all your goals without requiring a ton of effort.

PLANTING COMPACT PLANTS

Once your plant babies are home from the garden center, it's time to put them into the ground. Planting compact plants is really no different than planting their full-sized kin, though if you're new to gardening, you may question whether or not your technique is up to par. To cover all our bases, let's discuss the best planting technique for each of the three types of hardy compact plants discussed in this book: perennials, shrubs, and trees.

I'll leave you to your own devices when it comes to planting the last group of compact plants covered in a later chapter: fruits and vegetables. There are many books dedicated to the topic of starting seeds and vegetable gardening, so I'll not dive into the subject here. Plus, many of the vegetable seed companies mentioned in the source list at the end of the book also have planting information on their websites.

Before I get to the actual process of planting, it's worth taking the time to explain **the importance of root loosening** when planting potted perennials, trees, and shrubs. It's a critical step in all of the following highlighted processes.

Plants that have been growing in a container for a long time are often potbound, which means their roots are growing in a circular fashion around the inside of the pot. In order for that plant to be successfully transplanted into the garden, the circling roots must first be loosened and untangled. If you skip this step, the roots could end up girdling (strangling) the plant, and they'll be reluctant to spread out into the existing soil to access nutrients and water.

Root loosening is done by teasing the roots apart with your fingers, but if the plant is very potbound, a pair of pruners, a scissors, or even a pruning saw is needed to cut through the roots and loosen them. Regardless of which method is used, don't be afraid to get a little aggressive. It's better to cut the roots out of their pot shape vigorously than be too gentle with the process and leave them in the form of a perfect cylinder. The same is true whether planting potbound trees, shrubs, or perennials.

HOW TO PLANT A COMPACT PERENNIAL

Though dormant bare-root perennials (meaning with no soil on their roots) are available in the late winter or early spring via various mail-order sources, the vast majority of perennials are sold potted in containers. In some cases, the plant has been growing in the pot for only a few weeks, while in other cases, especially close to the end of the growing season, it's been in the pot for several months.

Regardless of how established the plant is in its pot, start by digging the properly sized hole. Aim for a hole size of approximately twice as wide as the plant's current spread. The depth of the hole should be exactly as deep as the root mass of the plant and no deeper. Planting perennials too deeply results in plant crowns that slip below the soil surface as they settle into their new home, yielding a bad case of crown rot and perhaps even death.

Toss a few shovels full of organic compost onto the top of the mound of backfill soil or work it into the entire planting area before digging the hole. Compost is a great soil amendment that adds not only plant nutrients to the area but also beneficial soil microbes, in addition to improving the soil's structure.

Slip the plant out of its pot, being careful not to snap off any top growth. Inspect the roots carefully and loosen them as described previously before placing the plant in the center of the hole and backfilling it with the compost-amended soil.

Settle the soil back into the hole and around the plant's roots by tamping it in with the palms of your hands. When planting is complete, the crown of the plant should sit exactly at ground level, not too deep and not too shallow. Readjust the plant if necessary.

Once the soil has been replaced, water the plant in well, soaking the root zone repeatedly. Don't worry about overwatering your perennials at planting time; any excess irrigation water will drain away with a little time. Keep the plants regularly watered until they're established, about 6 to 12 months later.

HOW TO PLANT A COMPACT SHRUB

Compact shrubs are primarily purchased growing in pots or with their root ball wrapped in burlap and twine (called balled and burlapped). Some shrubs may be available bare-root through mail order sources, but this is much less common.

POT-GROWN SHRUBS: When planting a compact shrub grown in a pot, begin by digging a hole two to three times as wide as the pot, but no deeper. Much like perennials, shrubs that are planted too deeply or too shallowly have a reduced chance of success. As you're digging, loosen the soil that comes out of the hole by breaking up any large chunks. Also, be sure to rough up the sides of the planting hole with a cultivator or shovel, especially if the soil contains a lot of clay. Slick sides in the planting hole make it hard for the roots to penetrate as they grow.

Once the hole is prepared, tip the shrub out of its container and loosen the roots as described on page 36.

Set the plant into the hole, making sure the root ball sits at the proper depth, and backfill with the soil that came out of the hole. While some recommend amending the backfill with compost, most of the existing research indicates that your best bet is to backfill with whatever soil came out of the hole. This helps the shrub better adjust to the existing soil conditions and keeps the roots from circling around in the planting hole. Water it in well and continue to regularly irrigate it for the first year after planting.

BALLED-AND-BURLAPPED SHRUBS: If your compact shrub came balled and burlapped, follow the preceding hole-digging instructions and then set the entire root ball—burlap and all—down in the hole. Once you confirm that the depth of the hole matches the depth of the root ball, untie and remove all the twine from around the plant. Then, use scissors to cut away all the burlap except for the small circle of it that sits beneath the root ball at the bottom of the hole.

After all the twine and most of the burlap have been removed, it's time to backfill the hole with the soil that was taken out of it, being sure to break up any large chunks along the way. Step the soil down into the hole to ensure no air pockets are left behind.

After backfilling the planting hole, spread a 1- to 2-inch-thick layer of shredded bark mulch or arborist wood chips around the base, being careful to keep it a few inches away from the bottom of the stems of the shrub. Essentially, create a doughnut of mulch around the shrub and over its root zone.

Water the shrub in well by setting the hose on a trickle and leaving it at the base of the plant for a few hours. The water seeps in slowly and thoroughly waters both the root ball and the surrounding soil. Keep the shrub well watered until it's established, about a year later.

HOW TO PLANT A COMPACT TREE

Like shrubs, compact trees are available either in pots or balled and burlapped. Some trees, primarily fruit-bearing types, are also available bare-root during the late winter and early spring. Here's the lowdown on the planting steps necessary for each of these three options.

POT-GROWN TREES: Trees grown in pots can be a struggle to get established, particularly if they're very potbound. It's absolutely essential that you dig a big planting hole that's at least three times the width of the pot, but no deeper. If you don't want to take a measuring tape out to the garden, use the handle of your shovel to compare the depth and width of the pot to the size of the planting hole.

Be extra sure to loosen or trim off any roots that were circling around inside the pot, and carefully inspect the base of the trunk to make sure no roots have begun to wrap around it. If you find one, simply cut it away with a sharp pair of pruners.

On seriously potbound trees, I sometimes use a pressure washer set on low or a sharp stream of water from the hose to remove every bit of soil from the roots, leaving behind just the roots, which can then be teased apart and spread out into the planting hole. This technique isn't easy, but it's one I've had good success with for very potbound trees. If you do this, you may still have to trim off a few roots, but you'll find the roots establish quickly, as long as the plant is well watered through the first 12 to 18 months after planting.

After placing the tree into the hole, backfill with the same soil that was removed, being sure to break up any large clods prior to filling the hole. After planting, the natural flare at the base of the tree's trunk must remain above soil level. If the tree was grafted and the graft union is clearly visible as a swollen knob at the base of the trunk, the site of the graft must stay several inches above the ground to prevent the root stock from sprouting any unwanted growth or suckers.

Make a doughnut of shredded bark mulch or arborist wood chips around the base of the tree, extending out to the tree's outermost branches. Keep the mulch from touching the base of the trunk. This deters bark-chewing rodents, insects, and rot.

Water the tree in well and continue to water regularly for at least a year.

BALLED-AND-BURLAPPED TREES: Planting a balled-and-burlapped tree is much the same as planting a balled-and-burlapped shrub, but with two important differences. Yes, the width of the planting hole should be three times the width of the root ball, but no deeper; and the twine and burlap should be cut away after the tree is situated in the planting hole. But, here's where the two differences come into play:

- First, if the tree's root ball was surrounded by a cage of wire, it's essential that you cut off and remove that cage with a wire cutter before backfilling the planting hole. Failure to do so could lead to strangled roots years after planting.

Planting a large balled-and-burlapped tree, like this one, is a challenging task. Be sure to remove the wire cage, twine, and the top section of the burlap prior to filling in the planting hole.

- Second, when you remove the burlap, if soil from the root ball is piled up against the base of the trunk such that the natural flare at the base of the tree's trunk is covered, clear the soil away with your fingers until the flare is fully exposed.

As with potted tree planting, be sure the knob of the graft union remains several inches above the ground if the tree is a grafted variety. Then, backfill with the same soil that came out of the hole, mulch the tree, and then water it in well.

BARE-ROOT TREES: Occasionally, trees are also available in bare-root form, meaning there's no soil on the roots and the trees are in a dormant state. Dwarf fruit and nut trees, as well as some compact ornamental trees, are often sold bare root.

Dwarf Alberta spruce are »
popular compact garden
plants often found growing
in containers at the nursery.
Planting them properly is
essential for the plant to thrive.

Prior to planting bare-root trees, soak their roots in a bucket of tepid water for 8 to 10 hours. Begin the planting process by carefully examining the base of the trunk for the soil line. You'll be able to see exactly how deeply the tree was planted in the field based on this line of soil. For grafted trees, it's typically several inches below the swollen graft union. That soil line is the depth to which the tree should be planted.

Dig a nice, wide hole and create a mound of soil at the bottom of it so the peak of the mound sits just below ground level. Place the bare-root tree on top of the mound and spread the roots out over the mound's sides. Backfill the hole with the soil that was removed from it. Be sure the soil line on the trunk sits level with the soil's surface in the new planting site, then press down the backfill soil with a hand or foot.

Create a doughnut of mulch around the tree and keep it well watered for the next 12 to 18 months or until it's established. There's no need to stake the tree unless the site is particularly windy or unstable.

Bare-root trees have no soil on their roots. At the nursery, they're stored at a temperature that keeps them in a state of dormancy. But, once they arrive on your doorstep, bare-root trees should be planted within a few days.

MAINTAINING COMPACT PLANTS

Though, as a whole, compact plants require less maintenance than their full-sized counterparts, there are some things to be done to keep these plants in tip-top shape. It's just good plant parenting to spend some time tending to your plants on a regular basis, even when they're as low maintenance as many compact varieties are. The following general maintenance chores are ones to add to your to-do list from time to time throughout the growing season, though other than watering, none of them are do-or-die tasks. If you skip pruning or fertilizing, it's likely that your plants will be no worse for the wear. They certainly won't die from it. That's what's so appealing about these plants, after all, their maintenance is amazingly minimal.

THE MAGIC 7 MAINTENANCE TASKS

Task #1: Watering (it's the only one you can't neglect!)

Of the seven maintenance tasks listed here, this is the only one that's absolutely essential. Plants, whether compact or not, cannot live without water; so this is the one maintenance task you cannot neglect. The trouble is, of course, that it's tough to determine exactly how much water to apply to a plant and how often to do it.

HOW MUCH WATER TO APPLY: Plants should always be watered in after planting by repeatedly soaking the soil around the base of the plant and allowing the water to percolate down to the root system. At planting time, it's pretty much impossible to overwater because any excess water will eventually drain away. But, the weeks and months after planting a new compact plant are also critical irrigation times to ensure proper plant establishment. More often than not, homeowners are prone to using the "splash-and-dash" method when watering their plants. They simply squirt some water on the plant itself using a hose or a sprinkler, and maybe get a little on the soil, and then call it a day. That is not good watering.

Watering is an ongoing task in any garden, but knowing how much and how often to water can be tricky.

Good watering involves applying enough water to thoroughly soak the entire root system and the surrounding soil. Deep watering encourages rapid root spreading and growth. For perennials, this means adding at least a gallon or two of water to each plant every time it's watered. For smaller trees and shrubs, 3 to 5 gallons is adequate; and for compact trees and shrubs that were in large containers, opt for 6 to 10 gallons of water per irrigation session. The water should be added slowly and in a gentle fashion (rather than via a sharp stream of water from the hose); it's better able to soak slowly into the soil and you'll lose less water to runoff.

Yes, roots need air; and if the soil is constantly wet, the roots can't breathe and the plant wilts and eventually dies. Waterlogged soil is a big no-no, especially when it comes to trees and shrubs planted in heavy clay soils. The trick, of course, comes in finding a balance. That coveted balance comes when you add the right amount of water at the right frequency.

HOW OFTEN TO WATER: Now that you know how much water to add to any particular plant, consider how often you should apply it. The frequency of irrigation depends on a number of different factors, including your soil type, the amount of sunlight the area receives, the size of the plant and its root zone, how thirsty the plant is, and how much natural rainfall has occurred.

Typically, newly planted specimens need more frequent watering than established plants do. Water can come from rain (invest in a good rain gauge and keep track) or from the end of your hose. For newly planted trees and shrubs, this means watering them with the appropriate amount of water every week to 10 days until they're established. For perennials, perhaps once or twice a week if no significant rainfall occurs. By the time a plant wilts, drought stress has already occurred. That stress can impact the health and future performance of that plant, so aim to water just before the symptoms of drought stress appear.

Once trees and shrubs are established a year or two after planting, they aren't nearly as dependent on you for irrigation. Except in cases of extreme drought, established trees and shrubs have root systems capable of accessing enough water on their own.

Task #2: Pruning

All of the compact plant varieties featured in this book require little, if any, pruning. In fact, if you want to skip this task completely, feel free to do so. But, there may be times when pruning is desired to either remove dead growth or improve flower or fruit production. Here are a few tips to help with the process:

1. Any time is a good time to prune out dead wood. Just be sure to use a sharp pair of clean pruners to avoid spreading any disease.

2. The pruning of trees and shrubs requires careful timing as follows:

   • For spring-flowering shrubs and trees that bloom on the previous year's growth, such as lilac, forsythia, azalea, and magnolia, prune immediately after bloom, as they typically form their flower buds the season before the flowers actually appear.

   • For summer-flowering shrubs and trees that bloom on growth produced earlier in the same season, such as spirea, rose-of–

Yearly pruning tasks are certainly reduced when growing compact varieties, but there will be times when a little haircut is necessary. Fruiting trees, shrubs, and vines are particularly in need of an annual pruning to increase vigor and production.

Sharon, buttonbush, and smoke bush, prune in the spring to encourage lush growth and a greater number of flower buds.

- For evergreen trees and shrubs that don't produce showy blooms, such as arborvitae, boxwood, junipers, and pines, pruning can be done anytime in the early spring, before new growth begins. You can also prune in the winter if you'd like to use the trimmings for holiday decorations.

- Most deciduous trees are best pruned in late winter through very early spring, when the tree is dormant. Maples and birches "bleed" a lot of sap when pruned in the late winter. Instead, trim these trees in the summer, though the loss of sap in the winter doesn't really harm the tree.

- Dwarf fruit trees and berry shrubs are best pruned during the dormant season, in late winter. Consult a fruit-pruning guide for how-to instructions on this important job. Proper pruning greatly affects fruit production and quality.

3. Avoid pruning shrubs and trees in late summer and early autumn, as new, late-season growth is susceptible to winter injury.

4. When pruning, be sure to keep your equipment clean. A spray of disinfectant on the blades should be used when moving from plant to plant to prevent the spread of disease.

Task #3: Deadheading

Deadheading is the removal of spent flowers, and while it isn't a necessary garden chore by any means, it improves the appearance and flower production of your plants, regardless of whether they're annuals, perennials, shrubs, or trees. Though each specific plant has slightly different deadheading needs, in general, this process is completed by trimming the spent flowers off the plant with a pair of garden shears. For perennials that produce a lot of tiny flowers, deadheading is best done with a pair of long-bladed loppers. For many plants, regular deadheading also increases future bloom production and keeps the plant in flower for months on end.

There are a few cases where you don't want to deadhead: in the berry patch, orchard, and vegetable garden, for example. There, the spent flowers will hopefully turn into fruits and veggies. Or, if you plan to save seeds from any of your plants, skip the task of deadheading.

Deadheading involves using a sharp pair of pruners or scissors to remove any spent flowers. This encourages the formation of new blooms.

Task #4: Mulching

Mulching is an important way to limit weed growth and reduce watering needs, though most compact plants will survive just fine without it. It also dresses up the garden and stabilizes soil temperature fluctuations. In most cases, a yearly layer of mulch between 2 and 3 inches thick is more than adequate. Which mulches to use around each particular planting area is up to the gardener's preferences, but here are some guidelines to get you started:

The best mulching material to use depends on the garden area you're caring for. Compost is a good choice for vegetable beds, but wood chips are an excellent choice for pathways and deeply rooted trees and shrubs.

- Shredded hardwood mulch, pine chips, arborist wood chips, and pine straw are excellent mulch choices for deeply rooted trees and shrubs. They break down more slowly than other mulches and really help hold in soil moisture.

- Straw, untreated grass clippings, compost, leaf mold, and shredded leaves are ideal for the vegetable garden, where they'll eventually break down into organic matter that can be turned into the soil to add plant nutrients and serve as food for beneficial soil microbes.

- Compost, mushroom soil, shredded leaves, and leaf mold are prime mulching choices for perennial flower beds. They help feed these fast-growing plants and limit competition from weeds.

Task #5: Fertilizing

Thankfully, the vast majority of compact plants require very little in terms of supplemental fertilization. Most are able to readily access the nutrients they need from the surrounding soil. There are, however, times when a good fertilization program boosts bloom power and plant performance.

- Nearly all compact evergreen plants, both broad-leaved and needled, as well as blueberries and camellias, prefer growing in soils with an acidic pH. Improper soil pH results in stunted growth and yellow leaves or needles (chlorosis), especially in the areas between the leaf veins. To make sure your soil pH is optimum, take a soil test every few years, either through an independent soil-testing laboratory or the extension service at your state's land-grant university. A fertilizer formulated specifically for acid-loving plants, such as Holly-tone®, is ideal for these plants.

- If you're finding that your compact flowering shrubs aren't producing blooms as planned, a soil test may indicate the need to add a balanced, complete fertilizer to the planting site.

- In the vegetable garden, fertile soil is key to good production, and so is maintaining a target pH of 6.5. A soil test (as described previously) is the only way to get an accurate assessment of your soil's pH, and since soil pH influences the availability of nearly every plant nutrient, it's an important number to know and adjust as necessary according to your test results. Most vegetables gain adequate nutrition from yearly additions of compost or aged animal manures, but a high-quality, granular organic fertilizer added to the beds also adds necessary nutrients if a soil test indicates the need.

The leaf yellowing on this birch tree indicates there's an issue with the health of the soil. Take a soil test to determine if the soil's pH is correct and if nutrient levels are adequate to support optimum plant growth.

Task #6: Winter protection

In some cases, protection from the elements during the winter months improves the health of certain trees and shrubs. If the site has high winter winds or heavy deer browse, it's beneficial to surround sensitive trees and shrubs with a fence of burlap or a layer of deer netting or fencing.

Protecting compact shrubs, such as this boxwood, from winter deer damage requires a layer of netting or fencing or the use of a deer-deterrent product.

Antidesiccant spray products are helpful if you're growing broad-leaved evergreen compact plants, like azaleas, laurels, boxwoods, and rhododendrons, and they're exposed to drying winter winds. These sprays are applied to the leaves in the early winter. They block the openings in the plant leaves and protect them from moisture loss, improving winter survival rates and reducing winter leaf burn.

Task #7: Yearly garden clean-up

If your garden contains a lot of perennials, an annual garden cleanup keeps things tidy. While it was once thought that the best time to do this chore was in the autumn, recent research shows that spring cleanups are best. Leave perennials and other plants standing in the garden for the winter to provide habitat for native bees, butterflies, and other beneficial insects, as well as birds and other wildlife. Cut back perennials and clean out garden beds as soon as the daytime temperatures are regularly in the 50s each spring. Compost the trimmings and shred the leaves to use them as mulch in your planting beds.

Winter is an important time for the wildlife living in your garden. Hold off on doing garden clean ups until the spring to provide habitat and shelter to bees, butterflies, beetles, and other beneficial insects.

For compact shrub and tree plantings, a spring garden cleanup primarily consists of raking out any autumn leaves that haven't blown over to the neighbor's house during the winter. That's it.

Though it might sound like a long list of gardening tasks to be done, keep in mind that ignoring or forgetting them from time to time does not spell certain death for your compact plants (with the exception of watering, of course). With time, you'll come to see that the limited maintenance needs of these small-statured plants definitely make a gardener's job easier. As always, it's important to be aware of your plants' health and what you might be able to do to improve it.

Now it's time to dive into the more creative aspects of gardening with compact plants and learn some great ways to include these plants in your own garden through design tips and landscape plans.

3

DESIGNING WITH COMPACT PLANTS

Using compact plants in the landscape presents homeowners with endless possibilities. While wide, sweeping gardens are lovely, so too are petite gardens, especially when they're filled with color, texture, and year-round interest. All the wonderful features of an enormous garden can be readily found in well-designed small-space gardens, too.

In truth, designing a small-scale garden is not all that different from creating a garden in a larger space, especially when it comes to remembering the basics, such as sun exposure, use, color, accessibility, and form. But, there are a few noticeable differences between the two.

DESIGNING A SMALL SPACE VS. A LARGE AREA

First, when designing a smaller garden, proper plant placement is a must. Utilize plants in a way that makes the space feel larger, not restrict the eye and block views. Compact plants are terrific for this task because they maintain their shape and size without becoming quickly overgrown. Adding a few vertical pops of upright growth among lower-growing plants lends a perception of depth to the garden and opens it up. The narrow, conical trees and evergreens found in chapters 4 and 5 are perfect for this job.

Also, using layers of plants is even more critical in small spaces than larger ones, as it enables the gardener to fit more plants into the area and to give a sense of depth even to the smallest of spaces. From trees that reach for the sky to groundcovers that hug the soil and every plant layer in between, make use of the vertical space available by designing a garden with multiple layers in play. Compact plants are so perfect for small gardens because they can be planted closer together. Creating these layers is, in some ways, simpler than it is in larger spaces where we're often tempted to plant things a little too close together.

And last, designing for accessibility is certainly easier in smaller spaces. Though compact plants in general require less maintenance than full-sized plants, you'll still have to get into the garden to weed, water, and prune from time to time. A well-designed small-scale garden plans for accessibility by including walkways and paths throughout.

DESIGN FOR LOW MAINTENANCE AND PLANT HEALTH

In addition to creating a lovely space, you also want a garden full of healthy plants. What's the use in having a well-designed garden if it's full of disease-ridden foliage that requires constant upkeep?

HERE ARE SOME TIPS FOR DESIGNING FOR LOW MAINTENANCE AND PLANT HEALTH:

- **Limit fungal diseases by properly spacing plants.** Yes, most compact varieties can be planted together fairly tightly, but do pay attention to the mature size of the plant and be sure you give it plenty of room to reach its full potential. Overcrowded plants are a welcome mat to fungal diseases.

- **Restrict weed growth by designing weeds out of the garden from the start.** Planting in layers readily accomplishes this. By including plenty of low-growing plants and groundcovers in a ground-level matrix, the soil is shaded. If done well, this serves as a sort of living mulch and prevents weeds from taking hold.

- **Include a diversity of plants in your small-scale garden to prevent major pest issues.** Several studies have shown that the greater the diversity of plant materials a garden has, the fewer pest outbreaks it faces. But, not to worry; including many different species of plants in your garden doesn't mean it has to be a jumbled mash-up of plants. By judiciously planning the placement of each plant prior to planting, a thoughtful, cohesive, and beautiful garden is the result.

DESIGN FOR COMFORT, MYSTERY, AND VISUAL EXPANSION

A sense of the unknown makes a garden appear to be larger than it is. When a visitor comes to your garden, they should wonder what's around the corner or where a path will take them, even if your garden is pint sized. Whether it's a meandering path, a peek-a-boo hole cut into a gate, a window made of mirrors placed on a shed wall, or a tiny playhouse tucked into the corner of the yard, there are many ways to add a sense of mystery to a small garden.

When designing a garden of compact plants, be sure to include plenty of places for rest and relaxation.

Open views, if you have them, should be accentuated. Create a "garden room" in these areas to give visitors pause and encourage them to stop and enjoy the view, even though they're in a confined space.

And last, include plenty of "living space" in your garden. A bistro table and chairs, a well-placed bench, or a patio sofa add comfort and personality to your small garden. Don't be afraid to include a pop of color or funk with these features; it's a great way to stylize the space.

Despite all of these tips and endless internet and Pinterest ideas at your fingertips, many gardeners still find themselves overwhelmed at the thought of designing a garden space, no matter how small. Turning to a professional designer is always a good idea, especially if design isn't your cup of tea. And so, to make the job easier, I've brought in some experts for the rest of this chapter—experts who make their living designing gardens of every shape and size.

I invited ten garden design professionals from all around North America to create a small-scale garden design with an accompanying plant list. Whether you use these plans as inspiration to come up with your own design or use their exact design right down to the last dwarf hydrangea, I hope they help you create the small-scale garden of your dreams.

SMALL-SCALE GARDEN DESIGNS FROM THE EXPERTS

Compact perennial garden

By Austin Eischeid

This modular perennial garden design was created for an 18' × 18' space, though it's easily repeated as a "stamp" for use in larger spaces. Feel free to cut it in half or even quarters if your space is more restricted. The plants found in this garden will survive down to −20°F.

The compact perennials chosen for this design are all known for their resilient nature, colorful blooms, and minimal maintenance requirements. It's designed for use in any full-sun area. From a mailbox garden to a patio planting, this compact perennial garden offers many beautiful possibilities.

PLANT LIST

1. 5 *Perovskia atriplicifolia* 'Little Spire' (dwarf Russian sage)

2. 4 *Vernonia lettermannii* 'Iron Butterfly' (compact ironweed)

3. 6 *Rudbeckia fulgida* var. *sullivantii* 'Little Goldstar' (dwarf black-eyed Susans)

4. 11 *Amsonia* × 'Blue Ice' (blue star)

5. 11 *Sporobolus heterolepis* 'Tara' (dwarf prairie dropseed)

6. 7 *Nepeta* Junior Walker™ (compact catmint)

Austin Eischeid is a garden designer based in Chicago, Illinois. He specializes in dynamic, naturalistic, seasonally sensitive, and low-maintenance landscapes. He is currently working on designs to renovate the landscape at Chicago's Millennium Park. See more of his work at www.AustinEischeid.com.

Pocket-sized pollinator garden

By Helen Weis

Even gardeners with limited space play an important role in supporting pollinators. This delightful design combines bee- and butterfly-friendly flowering perennials and ornamental grasses, backed by a small flowering tree, to bring insect life to the landscape. Requiring just a 12' × 12' quarter-circle of land, this colorful garden is packed with blooms and perfect for a front- or backyard planting.

All of the plants found in this design are winter hardy down to −10°F, with many of them being winter hardy down to −20°F. The anchor of this garden is a chaste tree (*Vitex agnus-castus*) that reaches just 8 to 10 feet in height, has a shrubby growth habit, and produces spires of blooms.

PLANT LIST

1. 1 *Vitex agnus-castus* (chaste tree)
2. 4 *Echinacea* Supreme™ 'Flamingo' (coneflower)
3. 2 *Echinacea* Butterfly™ 'Rainbow Marcella' (dwarf coneflower)
4. 6 *Hemerocallis* 'Fashionably Late' (daylily)
5. 6 *Hemerocallis* 'Happy Returns' (dwarf daylily)
6. 2 *Agastache* × 'Arizona Sunset' (anise hyssop)
7. 4 *Solidago shortii* 'Solar Cascade' (short goldenrod)
8. 2 *Eutrochium dubium* 'Little Joe' (compact Joe-pye weed)
9. 3 *Liatris spicata* 'Kobold' (compact blazing star)
10. 4 *Salvia* × *sylvestris* 'May Night' (salvia)
11. 4 *Scabiosa columbaria* 'Butterfly Blue' (pincushion flower)
12. 2 *Asclepias tuberosa* (butterfly weed)
13. 3 *Leucanthemum* × *superbum* 'Snowcap' (compact Shasta daisy)
14. 2 *Agastache* 'Violet Vision' (anise hyssop)
15. 3 *Calamagrostis* × *acutiflora* 'Karl Foerster' (feather reed grass)
16. 8–10 *Phlox subulata* (creeping phlox)

Helen Weis is the owner of Unique by Design Landscaping & Containers, a boutique design firm in Edmond, Oklahoma. She is one of the top container designers in the industry and among Oklahoma's favorite perennial garden designers. Helen is well known in the landscape industry for her contributions to many national publications, including Fine Gardening *magazine, the Association of Professional Landscape Designers' quarterly magazine* The Designer, *and State-by-State Gardening's* Oklahoma Gardener, *in addition to several books. Find Helen at www.ubdlandscape.com.*

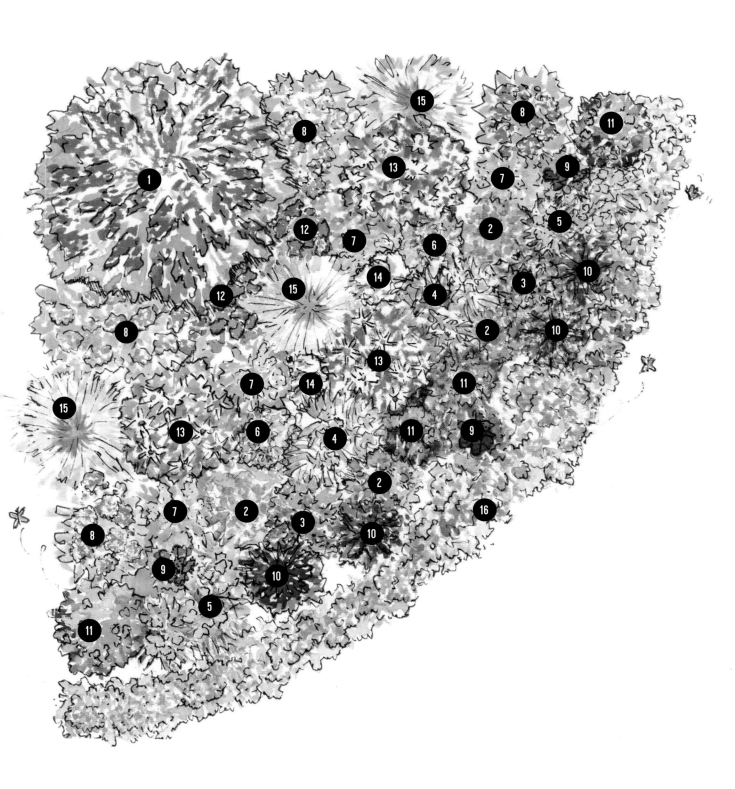

Patio garden with compact trees, shrubs, and perennials

By Naomi Brooks

Small backyards often come with even smaller outdoor living spaces. This design maximizes the potential of an area that's just 12' × 20' by surrounding a stone, brick, or concrete dining patio with flowering shrubs and perennials. The corner of the space is graced with a single, open-formed tree that won't take over the space or make visitors feel closed in.

All of the plants used in this plan are winter hardy down to −20°F, and none of the shrubs grow taller than 5 feet in height, with most staying shorter. The texture and bloom power of the shrubs in this design turn your patio into a backyard oasis.

PLANT LIST

1. 1 *Amelanchier × grandiflora* Autumn Brilliance® (serviceberry)
2. 2 *Clethra alnifolia* Sugartina® 'Crystalina' (compact summersweet)
3. 1 *Physocarpus opulifolius* Tiny Wine® (compact ninebark)
4. 1 *Sambucus racemosa* Lemony Lace® (cutleaf elderberry)
5. 3 *Hydrangea paniculata* Little Quick Fire® (dwarf panicle hydrangea)
6. 1 *Fothergilla gardenii* (dwarf fothergilla)
7. 1 *Caryopteris × clandonensis* Sapphire Surf™ (dwarf bluebeard)
8. 7 *Phlox paniculata* 'Jeana' (garden phlox)
9. 3 *Geranium* 'Rozanne' (perennial cranesbill)
10. 11 *Carex* 'Silver Sceptre' (Japanese sedge)

Naomi Brooks is a designer from the Hudson Valley of New York, where she helps to dream, design, and deliver uncommon outdoor spaces. She takes a crazy amount of photographs for her lectures to illustrate how the geometry of architecture and the patterns in our natural landscapes can be incorporated into garden designs. Find Naomi and her company, Verdant Landscapes, online at www.verdantlandscapes.com.

Tex-Mex courtyard garden for dry climates

By Jenny Peterson

This stunning Tex-Mex courtyard garden is perfect for dry climates. The plants found in it require little irrigation, and the garden is filled with plants that shine in arid regions. Surrounded on three sides by a wall, the 36' × 21' design has a fountain and a seating area. Star jasmine climbs the walls, while a slow-growing sago palm anchors each corner.

Each of the planting beds in this design is surrounded with a low, 18-inch-tall stucco wall to hold the soil and mulch in place, but other materials could be used as well. Though most of the plants in this garden will not survive the winters where temperatures dip below freezing, it's ideal for areas with warm, dry winters.

PLANT LIST

1. 1 *Bauhinia lunarioides* (Anacacho orchid tree)
2. 2 *Artemisia schmidtiana* 'Silver Mound' (Angel's Hair artemisia)
3. 3 *Trachelospermum jasminoides* (star jasmine)
4. 16 *Dianella tasmanica* 'Variegata' (striped dianella)
5. 3 *Salvia leucantha* 'Santa Barbara' (Mexican bush sage)
6. 2 *Asclepias tuberosa* (butterfly weed)
7. 7 *Nassella tenuissima* (Mexican feather grass)
8. 1 *Tagetes lucida* (Mexican mint marigold)
9. 15 *Sedum mexicanum* (Mexican sedum)
10. 3 *Echinacea purpurea* 'Lilliput' (compact coneflower)
11. 20 *Verbena canadensis* 'Homestead Purple' (creeping verbena)
12. 1 *Caesalpinia pulcherrima* (red bird of paradise)
13. 2 *Rosmarinus officinalis* 'Blue Boy' (compact rosemary)
14. 4 *Cycas revoluta* (sago palm)

FOR CONTAINERS

15. 2 *Echinocactus grusonii* (golden barrel cactus); and 2 *Dichondra argentea* 'Silver Falls' (Silver ponyfoot)

Jenny Peterson is an Austin, Texas–based landscape designer, author, and speaker focusing on wellness and healing gardens. She is the author of The Cancer Survivor's Garden Companion: Cultivating Hope, Healing and Joy in the Ground Beneath Your Feet, *which received the Silver Award from the Association for Garden Communicators. Find Jenny at www.JennyNybroPeterson.com, where she writes about healthy gardens, healthy lives, and urban farming.*

Small-scale front entrance garden

By Sue Goetz

Dressing up your home's front entrance is one of the easiest ways to add value and interest to your property. The small-statured plants included in this lovely entrance garden are not just the perfect fit; they're also wonderfully fragrant.

Flanking a casual walkway constructed of steppingstones or blocks, every shrub and perennial included in this garden welcomes guests and residents, alike, with a divine scent and colorful blooms. The area measures just 16' × 20', and all of the plants found in it are winter hardy down to at least 0°F.

PLANT LIST

1. 1 *Magnolia grandiflora* 'Little Gem' (dwarf southern magnolia)

2. 1 *Syringa pubescens sub. patula* 'Miss Kim' (dwarf Korean lilac)

3. 5 *Abelia × grandiflora* 'Confetti' (Confetti® flowering abelia)

4. 2 *Rosa* 'Vineyard Song' (shrub rose)

5. 1 *Daphne × transatlantica* 'Blafra' Eternal Fragrance™ (daphne)

6. 2 *Euonymus japonicus* 'Green Spire' (upright euonymus)

7. 6 *Lavandula angustifolia* 'Hidcote' (English lavender)

8. 8 *Dianthus gratianopolitanus* 'Tiny Rubies' (cheddar pinks)

9. 6 *Geranium × cantabrigiense* 'Karmina' (cranesbill)

10. 8–10 *Thymus serpyllum* 'Elfin' (elfin thyme)

11. 1 potted *Trachelospermum jasminoides* grown as an annual (star jasmine)

Sue Goetz is a garden designer, writer, and speaker from Tacoma, Washington. Through her business, Creative Gardener, she works with clients to personalize outdoor spaces. Her design work has earned gold medals, the Sunset Magazine Award, and the Fine Gardening award at the Northwest Flower & Garden Show. Sue is also a passionate herb gardener and the author of The Herb Lover's Spa Book *and* A Taste for Herbs. *Find Sue online at www.thecreativegardener.com.*

Shady nook of compact plants

By Jan Coppola Bills

Shady garden areas are among the most challenging for gardeners. While brightly hued blooms often play second fiddle in a shade garden, the real standouts are perennials, shrubs, and trees with colorful foliage and interesting textures or forms.

For this near-symmetrical shade garden, the designer combined multiple leaf textures together to create a cool, calming space meant to flank a walkway or garden path. Plant this 21' × 23' shady nook at the front or rear of a home or next to a patio or deck. All the plants found in this garden require fewer than 4 hours of sun per day and are winter hardy down to −20°F.

PLANT LIST

1. 1 *Acer palmatum* 'Wolff' Emperor I® (Emporer Japanese maple)

2. 6 *Hakonechloa macra* 'All Gold' (Japanese forest grass)

3. 6 *Taxus cuspidata* 'Monloo' Emerald Spreader® (Japanese Yew)

4. 6 *Hydrangea macrophylla* 'All Summer Beauty' (mophead hydrangea)

5. 6 *Heuchera micrantha* 'Palace Purple' (coralbells)

6. 6 *Hosta* × 'Golden Tiara' (hosta)

7. 6 *Hosta* × 'Blue Angel' (hosta)

8. 12 *Athyrium niponicum* var. *pictum* (Japanese painted fern)

9. 11 *Athyrium filix-femina* var. *angustum* 'Lady in Red' (lady fern)

Jan Coppola Bills is the author of Late Bloomer, *a certified landscape designer, advanced Master Gardener, entrepreneur, and contributing writer for State-by-State Gardening magazines. After a successful career in the corporate world, she made a major life reassessment and followed her heart: She traded in her heels for Wellies and started the Detroit-area landscape design company, Two Women and a Hoe® (www.twowomenandahoe.com).*

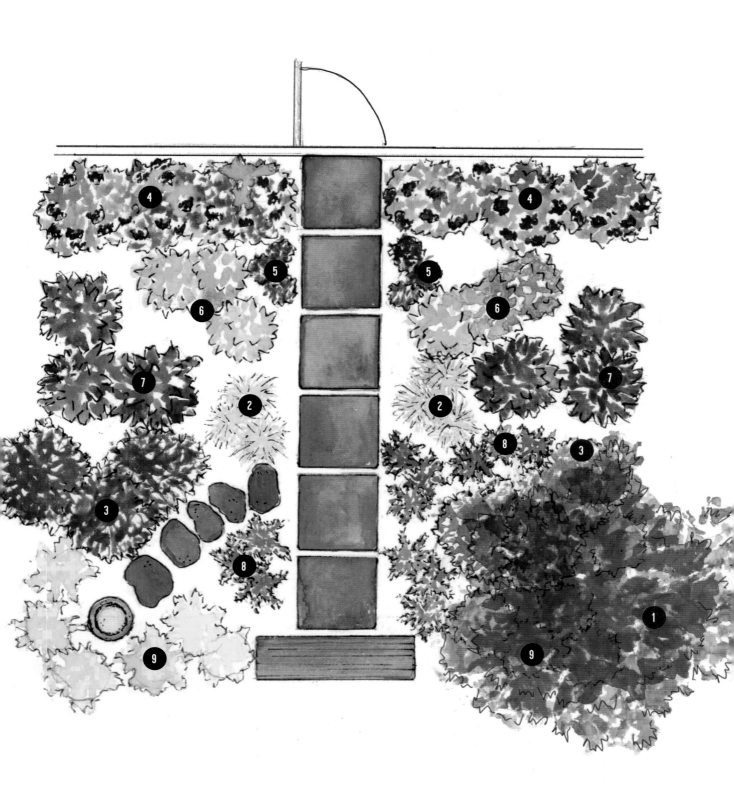

Backdoor cocktail garden

By Jennifer R. Bartley

Cocktail gardens are a place to sit, relax, and unwind—especially during the evening hours—but they can also include plants used to make or embellish a beverage. This unique backdoor cocktail garden includes a nook near the house to sit and sip as well as a circular stone overlook with a seatwall for socializing with friends and family.

This large design is filled with woodland plants that include many North American natives and edible plants such as pawpaw, elderberry, gooseberry, clove currant, and pink currant. The space measures 56' × 48', but it can easily be scaled down for smaller backyards. All of the plants found in this design are winter hardy down to at least −20°F.

PLANT LIST

1. 1 *Amelanchier lamarckii* (Juneberry)
2. 1 *Aronia melanocarpa* 'Autumn Magic' (black chokeberry)
3. 1 *Asimina triloba* 'Sweet Alice' (pawpaw)
4. 1 *Asimina triloba* 'Wells' (Wells pawpaw)
5. 3 *Ceanothus americanus* (New Jersey tea)
6. 3 *Cornus florida* 'Cherokee Brave' (dogwood)
7. 1 *Hamamelis virginiana* 'Champlin's Red' (witch hazel)
8. 3 *Hydrangea quercifolia* 'Pee Wee' (dwarf oakleaf hydrangea)
9. 3 *Lindera benzoin* (spicebush)
10. 1 *Ptelea trifoliata* (hop tree)
11. 1 *Ribes* 'Poorman' (gooseberry)
12. 2 *Ribes odoratum* 'Crandall' (American clove currant)
13. 2 *Ribes rubrum* 'Gloire des Sablons' (compact pink currant)
14. 1 *Sambucus canadensis* 'Nova' (American elderberry)
15. 1 *Sambucus canadensis* 'York' (American elderberry)
16. 4 *Aralia racemosa* (American spikenard)
17. 11 *Aruncus dioicus* 'Kneiffii' (dwarf goatsbeard)
18. 15 *Asarum canadense* (wild ginger)
19. 11 *Carex pensylvanica* (Pennsylvania sedge)
20. 10 *Dryopteris erythrosora* 'Brilliance' (autumn fern)
21. 12 *Galium odoratum* (sweet woodruff)
22. 16 *Geranium maculatum* (wild geranium)
23. 10 *Helleborus orientalis* (Lenten rose)
24. 4 *Hosta* 'Halcyon' (compact blue hosta)
25. 1 *Lamprocapnos spectabilis* 'Alba' (white bleeding heart)
26. 6 *Matteuccia struthiopteris* (ostrich fern)
27. 6 *Panax quinquefolius* (American ginseng)
28. 10 *Phlox divaricata* (woodland phlox)
29. 7 *Podophyllum peltatum* (mayapple)
30. 15 *Polygonatum biflorum* (Solomon's seal)
31. 3 *Polystichum acrostichoides* (Christmas fern)
32. 10 *Rhus aromatica* 'Gro-Low' (dwarf fragrant sumac)

Jennifer R. Bartley traveled extensively throughout France to study traditional potagers (kitchen gardens) and has created her own versions for American chefs and gardeners. Emphasizing functionality and design in her work, Jennifer seeks to create beautiful, vibrant gardens that embrace a simpler life. A landscape architect in Granville, Ohio, Jennifer is also the author of Designing the New Kitchen Garden *and* The Kitchen Gardener's Handbook. *Find her online at www.americanpotager.com.*

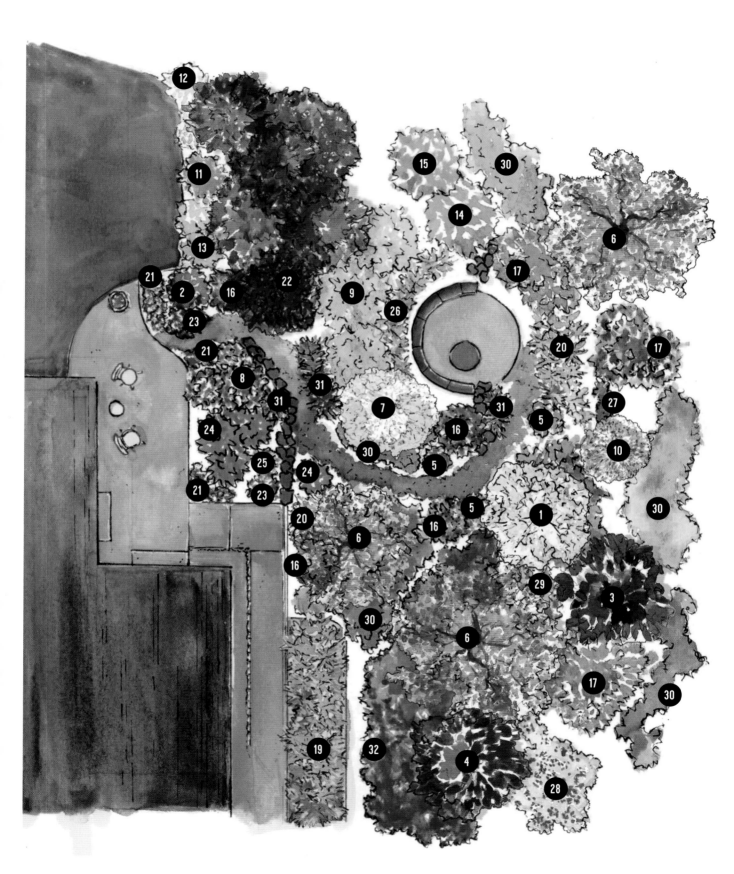

Mini herb garden of compact varieties

By Niki Jabbour

This beautiful little all-in-one herb garden includes culinary herbs, tea herbs, and edible flowers. The space is only 6' × 6', so it's a great way for a beginner gardener or anyone with limited space to grow a selection of herbs. Designed to be grown in a raised bed made from wooden boards, the central diamond is also made from a wooden frame. Raise it to a second level or keep it on-level with the outer bed frame.

While there are some perennial herbs in this garden (including thyme, oregano, lavender, and chives), the remaining herbs will not survive the winter where temperatures dip below freezing. For this reason, the frost-sensitive herbs, such as basil, dill, lemongrass, parsley, and nasturtiums, need to be replaced each spring.

PLANT LIST

1. 3 *Petroselinum crispum* 'Wega' (dwarf curly parsley)
2. 3 *Thymus citriodorus* (lemon thyme)
3. 2 *Origanum vulgare* var. *hirtum* (Greek oregano)
4. 1 *Lavandula angustifolia* 'Munstead' (Munstead lavender)
5. 3 *Ocimum basilicum* 'Dolce Fresca' (compact sweet basil)
6. 3 *Allium schoenoprasum* 'Fine Leaf' (fine leaf chives)
7. 1 *Artemisia dracunculus* (French tarragon)
8. 2 *Rosmarinus officinalis* 'Arp' (rosemary)
9. 1 *Cymbopogon citratus* (lemongrass)
10. 3 *Ocimum basilicum* 'Spicy Globe' (dwarf globe basil)
11. 2 *Anethum graveolens* 'Fernleaf' (dwarf dill)
12. 2 *Tropaeolum majus* 'Dwarf Jewel Mix' (mounding nasturtium)

Niki Jabbour is a garden writer from Halifax, Nova Scotia, whose books include The Year-Round Vegetable Gardener *and* Veggie Garden Remix. *She is also the host of* The Weekend Gardener *radio show and writes regularly for magazines and newspapers like* Fine Gardening, Horticulture, *and* Birds & Blooms. *Find Niki online at www.savvygardening.com.*

Balcony container foliage garden

By Christina Salwitz

For those with extremely limited growing space, containers are a wonderful option for growing compact plants. This simple yet lovely container design comes from an expert who specializes in creating unique container displays that utilize interesting and varied textures and foliage colors. Use it to dress up a small city balcony, a front or back porch, or an apartment courtyard.

The combination of prized foliage plants included in this design is perfect for any garden pot with a rim diameter of at least 12 inches across. Whether made from glazed ceramic, fiberglass, plastic, or another material, as long as the container is at least 18 inches deep and is regularly watered throughout the growing season, the plants will thrive. Though several of the varieties found in this design will not survive the winter where temperatures drop below freezing, the container is easy to replant at the start of each growing season.

PLANT LIST

1. 1 *Cordyline australis* 'Red Star' (dracaena palm)
2. 1 *Carex oshimensis* 'Everillo' Evercolor® (Evercolor carex)
3. 1 *Thymus citriodorus* (lemon thyme)
4. 1 *Hedera helix* 'Midget' (miniature English ivy)

Christina Salwitz is a personal garden coach, container garden designer, and public speaker in Renton, Washington. As coauthor of Fine Foliage *and* Gardening with Foliage First, *Christina provides every level of gardener with a fresh and objective perspective on their special needs. She's appeared in and written for magazines such as* Better Homes & Gardens, Fine Gardening, *and* Horticulture. *Learn more about Christina on her website, www.personalgardencoach.wordpress.com.*

Kitchen garden with compact edible plants

By Ellen Ecker-Ogden

Kitchen gardens are naturally designed to be smaller than a typical vegetable garden. They're the perfect place to grow herbs, greens, vegetables, and edible flowers. This garden is meant to be located just outside the kitchen door, so the cook can easily dash outside to clip a few leaves for a salad or vegetables for the pot.

Measuring just 18' × 18', the garden is constructed of four square beds and four rectangular ones. The bed areas can be at ground level or they can be raised beds constructed of wood, brick, or blocks. Filled with compact vegetable varieties and flowers that fit perfectly into the small beds and still produce ample food, this garden is centered with a large pot filled with dwarf sweet peas. With the exception of the tomatoes, which should be planted into the garden as 4- to 6-week-old transplants, the vegetables and flowers found in this garden are easily grown from seed planted directly into the garden in most growing zones.

PLANT LIST

1. 24 'Peach Melba' nasturtium
2. 24 'Italian White' sunflower
3. 10 'Peas-in-a-Pot' sweet peas
4. 48 'Sugar Snap' peas
5. 25 'French Mascotte' bush bean
6. 6 'Lemon Cucumber' cucumber
7. 8 'Red Profusion' tomato
8. 18 'Baby' pak choi
9. 32 'Little Hero' spinach
10. 3 'Honey Bear' winter squash
11. 14 'Little Gem' lettuce
12. 18 'Rainbow' swiss chard
13. 36 'Chantenay' carrots
14. 48 '18 Day' radish ('De 18 Jours')
15. 12 'Lemon Gem' marigold

Ellen Ecker Ogden is a kitchen garden designer and author of The Complete Kitchen Garden *and* The New Heirloom Garden. *As a student of classic garden design, she gains much of her inspiration from European potagers and lectures widely on her love of growing beautiful food. You can find Ellen online at www.ellenogden.com.*

Though these design plans include many wonderful compact plant varieties, there are so many more available to gardeners. As you're about to see, compact plants are perfect not just for beautifying outdoor spaces and providing edible fruits and vegetables for the family; they're also good at overcoming various challenges in the landscape. Next, let's take a look at a few ways that compact plants can make even your worst gardening woes disappear.

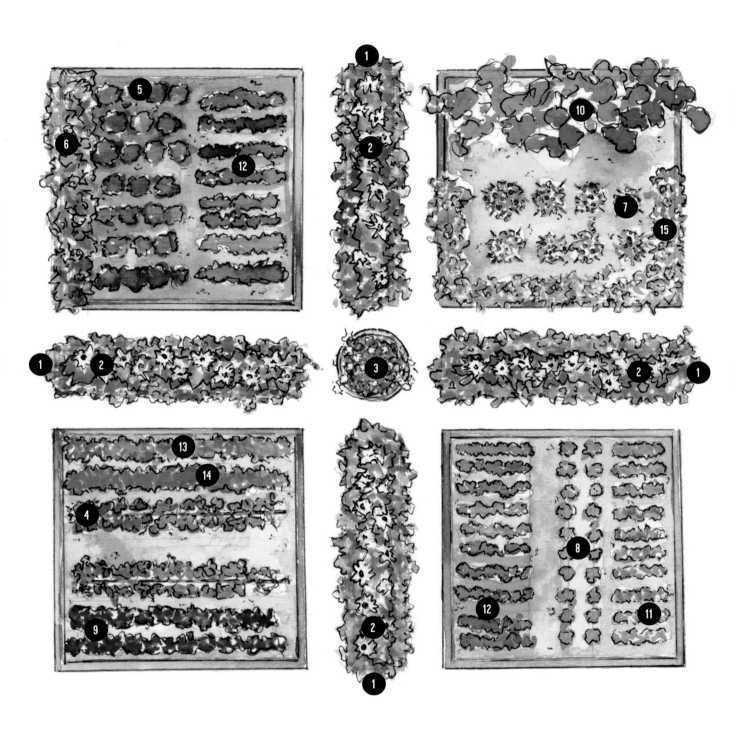

4

COMPACT PLANTS WITH PURPOSE

From time to time, gardeners may come across a particular garden area that presents them with a real challenge. Perhaps it's because the growing conditions are less than ideal. Or, maybe it's because the site is sloped and difficult to access. Or, maybe there's a gem of a neighbor who piles their junk right on the property line. Lots of different areas can prove problematic for gardeners. It costs time and money to try to remedy these issues, but in many cases, solving the problem comes down to choosing the best plants for the job.

There's a common saying among garden professionals: "Right plant, right place." In essence, the expression is meant to stress the importance of selecting the right plants for each particular garden space and the growing conditions it offers. But, when the "right place" has subpar growing conditions or there's some other difficult issue to overcome, gardeners have to work extra hard to find the "right plant" for the job. That's where this chapter can help.

In this problem-solving chapter, eight common landscaping challenges are presented, followed by brief descriptions and photos of a handful of the very best compact plant varieties to help remediate these troublesome issues. Use these lists to select the right compact plants for your needs and get a handle on whatever gardening challenges come your way. In subsequent chapters, you'll find many more compact plants via in-depth profiles. As you read those profiles, you're likely to discover even more plants with problem-solving attributes you can add to the list.

CHALLENGE #1: A BORING WINTER LANDSCAPE

Winter gardens are all too often devoid of color and structure. In the throes of the summer gardening season, we forget to consider what the garden will look like in the dead of winter; we're too busy enjoying the fragrances and colors of flowering perennials and annuals to think about snow days. But when the blooms are gone, it's important to have plants in the garden that capture the eye. Whether they have an evergreen growth habit, interesting bark, colored twigs, a unique form, beautiful berries, or some other winter attribute, these compact plants can help overcome a dull and boring winter landscape.

Compact plants to provide winter interest

1. SHERWOOD COMPACT MUGO PINE (*PINUS MUGO* 'SHERWOOD COMPACT'): This very hardy evergreen pine is a true dwarf that has a mounded shape and candelabra-like branch growth. Its stems are covered with long needles, and a slow growth rate means no pruning is necessary to maintain the optimum size and shape. 'Sherwood Compact' reaches just 2 to 3 feet tall and wide and is winter hardy down to −50°F.

2. SOFT TOUCH INKBERRY (*ILEX CRENATA* 'SOFT TOUCH'): 'Soft Touch' holly is winter hardy down to −20°F. It's a mounded shrub that maxes out at just 2 to 3 feet tall and wide and requires little to no pruning; it's perfect for tiny backyards. The foliage is dark green, and the small leaves make a lovely addition to the garden year round. Unlike some other hollies, 'Soft Touch's' leaves do not have spines; their edges are soft and rounded.

3. VANDEN AKKER WEEPING ALASKA CEDAR (*CHAMAECYPARIS NOOTKATENSIS* 'VAN DEN AKKER'): Skinny is the best word to describe this columnar tree for small yards and gardens. The thinnest of all the weeping Alaska cedars, it reaches 20 feet tall but is only 1 foot wide! The short, tight branches weep, while the central trunk grows straight up. This extremely narrow evergreen tree has soft, fan-like growth and is a truly unique addition to any compact garden space. Winter hardy down to −20°F.

4. COMPACT CRANBERRY BUSH (*VIBURNUM TRILOBUM* 'COMPACTUM'): This cultivar of the North American native cranberry bush, *viburnum* offers year-round interest. The new spring growth is tinged in red. It's then followed by white, flat-topped flower clusters that form clusters of bright red berries in the fall. A quick growth rate means the 6-foot height and width is reached within a few years. Birds love the berries on this shrub, and it's winter hardy down to −50°F.

5. MAGICAL® PINK CARPET SNOW BERRY (*SYMPHORICARPOS* 'KOLMPICA'): An

eye-catching beauty that shrugs off winters down to −30°F, this compact form of snow berry produces flowers in May and June. The blooms are followed by clusters of pink, chubby berries on the branch tips. Great for both containers and in-ground gardens, and topping out at just 3 feet tall and wide, Magical® Pink Carpet is nothing short of adorable.

6. LITTLE GOBLIN® WINTERBERRY HOLLY (*ILEX VERTICILLATA* 'NCIV1'):

Winterberry hollies lose their leaves in the autumn, exposing densely packed, deep red berries on every branch that persist well into the winter. You'll need a pollinator variety such as Little Goblin® Guy for this dwarf female shrub to produce berries. One male for every five female plants is ideal. Topping out at 3 to 5 feet with an equal spread, Little Goblin® can handle even damp, poorly drained soils and is winter hardy down to −40°F.

7. TWISTY BABY™ DWARF BLACK LOCUST (*ROBINIA PSEUDOACACIA* 'LACE LADY'):

The winter interest this tree offers is in the form of its contorted branches. A great specimen plant for a small garden or container, the unique twisted branches reach up to 10 to 15 feet in height, but you can prune to keep it smaller if needed. This deciduous tree's leaves and leaf stems are curvy and twisty, too, with a hint of silver on their undersides. In spring, Twisty Baby™ is covered with drooping panicles of fragrant white flowers. Winter hardy down to −30°F.

8. GOLDEN TUFTED HAIR GRASS (*DESCHAMPSIA CESPITOSA* 'GOLDTAU'): The

compact habit, long bloom time, and golden-yellow flower stalks, make this grass a garden champ. Tussocks of deep green foliage reach 1 to 2 feet tall and 2 to 3 feet wide. The airy flowers appear in summer and persist through the winter, providing interest and texture to the landscape. Winter hardy down to −30°F, golden tufted-hair grass tolerates hot and dry weather and is deer resistant, too.

CHALLENGE #2: A SLOPED SITE

I live in western Pennsylvania, where it's difficult to find a yard that doesn't have a slope. Level lots are tough to come by around here, and as a result, I'm often asked about the best way to handle a slope that's too steep to mow. The answer, of course, is to fill it with compact plants!

While unmowable slopes have traditionally been the realm of groundcovers like pachysandra, myrtle, and creeping sedum, times have changed. With the introduction of numerous dwarf evergreens, flowering shrubs, roses, and perennials comes the opportunity to create beautiful gardens on sloped sites instead of just slathering them with a single groundcover destined to be overrun with grass and weeds before it fills in. Mixing various compact plants together in a thoughtful design allows homeowners to turn a troublesome area into a beautiful garden, and because these plants stay naturally compact, there's no need to don your rock climbing gear to prune them every spring. As long as you can mulch the slope early in the season to limit weeds, these plants are fairly self-sustaining.

Compact plants to cover sloped sites

1. SHOW OFF® SUGAR BABY® FORSYTHIA (*FORSYTHIA × INTERMEDIA* 'NIMBUS'):
Winter hardy down to −20°F, this bright, compact forsythia has a lot to offer. Deer resistant with vase-shaped, pint-sized growth, Sugar Baby® produces canary yellow blooms on bare branches in very early spring. A slew of green, pest-proof leaves appear soon after. With a height and spread of 18 to 30 inches, this adaptable shrub makes a great slope cover.

2. COMPACT PLUME JUNIPER (*JUNIPERUS HORIZONTALIS* 'PLUMOSA COMPACTA'):
Yet another excellent small shrub, this feathery, blue-green dwarf juniper reaches only 2 feet in height with double the spread. It makes a great evergreen groundcover and looks lovely all winter long. Surviving winters down to −40°F, 'Plumosa Compacta' is no wimpy little plant.

3. WABI SABI® VIBURNUM (*VIBURNUM PLICATUM* VAR. *TOMENTOSUM* 'SMVPTFD'):
Topping out at just 2 to 3 feet in height, with an equal spread, Wabi Sabi® is a total doll. This dwarf version of the classic doublefile viburnum we all know and love is low and wide, making it perfect for covering slopes, lining walkways, and sprucing up foundation plantings. It's fairly shade tolerant, too. With strong horizontal growth, white, flat-topped spring flowers, and excellent fall color, there's not a single thing to dislike about this shrub. Winter hardy down to −20°F.

4. DWARF ENGLISH BOXWOOD (*BUXUS SEMPERVIRENS 'SUFFRUTICOSA'*): This dwarf boxwood is a prime garden plant for so many reasons. Its compact growth habit (it matures at just 2 to 3 feet tall and wide), slow growth rate, and impeccable form make it a great choice for small and large gardens, alike. The deer-resistant foliage does need some protection from strong winter winds to avoid winter dieback where winters are very cold, but it's fully winter hardy down to −20°F. The evergreen, glossy leaves are 1 inch long and quite dense along the stems.

5. DRIFT® ROSES (*ROSA HYBRID* DRIFT® SERIES): If ever there were a rose to overcome challenging sites in small gardens, the Drift® rose is it! With nine different available varieties, this 2-feet-tall and 3-feet-wide rose comes in a wide range of colors. Its spreading growth habit makes it perfect for mass plantings or for use as a groundcover. The disease-resistant foliage produces repeated clusters of blooms every 5 to 6 weeks, all season long. There's no need to deadhead this rose, either. Just prune it hard in the early spring and then put your pruners away for the rest of the year. With a winter hardiness down to −20°F, this is a no-fail rose for small-space gardeners.

6. LITTLE GRAPETTE DAYLILY (*HEMEROCALLIS* 'LITTLE GRAPETTE'): Everyone loves reliable and tough-as-nails daylilies, right? While full-sized varieties may prove to be too large for smaller landscapes, 'Little Grapette' is right at home. A clump-former with slender, grass-like leaves, this 16-inch-tall daylily bears purple flowers with a yellow/green throat. It produces several flushes of new blooms throughout the growing season, so it's far from a one-trick pony. Winter hardy down to −30°F, 'Little Grapette' is ideal for mass and specimen plantings, alike.

7. JUNIOR WALKER™ CATMINT (*NEPETA × FAASSENII* 'NOVANEPJUN'): This compact catmint is a personal favorite for hot, dry, sloped gardens and perennial borders. Its maximum height is 18 inches with double the spread, making it ideal for covering a lot of ground in a very low-maintenance way. Smothered in purple-blue flower spikes in spring and summer, the fragrant, blue-tinged foliage is also deer and rabbit resistant. Winter hardy down to −20°F, Junior Walker™ is a favorite of bees and other pollinators. Plus, it's drought tolerant, too.

8. COMPACT PFITZER JUNIPER (*JUNIPERUS CHINENSIS* 'KALLAY'S COMPACT'): An improved, compact form of the Pfitzer juniper, 'Kallay's Compact' reaches just 3 feet tall and 6 feet wide. This evergreen is a vigorous grower with dense branching, which makes it great for a low hedge or slope planting. The horizontal-spreading branches are attractive year-round. Winter hardy down to −30°F, this evergreen is also said to be deer resistant.

CHALLENGE #3: AN UNSIGHTLY VIEW

Whether you're aiming to block the neighbor's pool or keep their poodle out of your yard, plants can solve your problem. The list of plants typically recommended for privacy screening and hedging includes some pretty large specimens that can quickly overtake a small backyard or urban landscape. While frequent pruning is one way to keep these plants more compact, there are better, lower-maintenance options now available to small-space gardeners. The varieties included here all have narrow growth habits, making them easy to space close together to create a privacy screen or hedge. Though a few of the plants I recommend here grow quite tall, most urban gardens are not "vertically challenged." There's plenty of room to grow up, so tall, narrow plants often work quite well. If that's not the case where you live, though, be sure to choose one of the shorter options.

Compact plants to provide privacy screening and hedging

1. SKY PENCIL HOLLY (*ILEX CRENATA* 'SKY PENCIL'): This narrow, upright evergreen is a smooth-leaved holly that reaches about 6 feet in height but is only 2 to 3 feet wide. Like other hollies, the male and female plants are separate. The females of this species produce tiny purple berries but only when a pollinating male plant is nearby. 'Sky Pencil' hollies are lovely trees for small gardens, and their evergreen growth habit means they provide winter interest, too. Winter hardy down to −20°F.

2. GREEN SPIRE EUONYMUS (*EUONYMUS JAPONICUS* 'GREEN SPIRE'): Winter hardy down to −10°F, 'Green Spire' euonymus is well behaved, giving it a more formal appearance than some other options. The glossy, green foliage is perfect for creating a narrow hedge or screen. Maxing out at 6 to 8 feet in height with a spread of just 1 to 2 feet, this naturally narrow shrub is a fast grower, too.

3. COLUMNAR SWEDISH ASPEN (*POPULUS TREMULA* 'ERECTA'): A thin cultivar of the Swedish aspen tree, this variety is an exceptional choice for slender garden areas and small yards. It's very cold hardy (down to −50°F) and has heart-shaped leaves that move in the wind. Though it's deciduous and loses its leaves in the winter, this columnar tree's structure is lovely even sans foliage. Its width is very limited, but it can grow up to 40 feet tall.

4. DAKOTA PINNACLE® BIRCH (*BETULA PLATYPHYLLA* 'FARGO'): The Dakota Pinnacle® birch is a columnar tree with leaves that turn a brilliant yellow in the fall and white, peeling bark. It's also resistant to the bronze birch borer, which is another definite plus. Among the most statuesque of all the columnar trees for small gardens, the Dakota Pinnacle® birch grows upwards of 25 feet tall at maturity but is only 8 to 10 feet wide. Winter hardy down to −40°F, this birch is lovely as both a specimen tree and, when planted close together, a privacy screen.

5. DWARF HORNBEAM (*CARPINUS BETULUS* 'COLUMNARIS NANA'): Though
hornbeams are fairly rigid, narrow trees to begin with, this variety is even
more well behaved. These winter hardy trees (down to −30°F) are like
perfect garden sculptures that reach only 6 feet tall at full maturity. The
slow growth rate of 'Columnaris Nana' means it takes a long time for
that to happen, which is yet another trait that makes this tree a must for
small gardens. Rich, medium green leaves grace the branches; they turn a
brilliant yellow in the autumn.

6. CRIMSON SPIRE™ OAK (*QUERCUS ROBUR* × *Q. ALBA* 'CRIMSCHMIDT'): This
unique oak tree is very tall—up to 40 feet—but it remains fairly narrow at
just 10 to 15 feet wide (yes, that's quite narrow for an oak!). The fall color
is exceptional. A stunning tree all around, but an especially valuable tree
for small gardens due to its ability to support a wide array of native insects
and the songbirds who eat them. Fully winter hardy down to −20°F,
several Crimson Spire™ oaks planted in a row make a striking privacy
screen or tall windbreak.

7. STANDING OVATION LITTLE BLUESTEM (*SCHIZACHYRIUM SCOPARIUM* 'STANDING OVATION'): Though this ornamental grass grows tall, its habit is quite
narrow, making it perfect for adding height to slender spaces. The
sturdy, upright stems are tinted blue with a hint of dark burgundy at
their base. With an excellent fall color and a winter hardiness down to
−40°F, 'Standing Ovation' is a vertical accent unlike any other. Silvery
flower stalks grace the plant in the late summer. Tolerant of lousy soils,
the only care this ornamental grass needs is to be cut down to a height
of 6 inches in the very early spring.

8. FEATHER REED GRASS (*CALAMAGROSTIS* × *ACUTIFLORA* 'KARL FOERSTER'):
Another ornamental grass for hedging and privacy screening, the narrow,
upright growth of 'Karl Foerster' has been a garden favorite for many
decades. Winter hardy down to −20°F, this grass reaches a height of 3 to 4
feet and a spread of 18 to 24 inches. The bright green leaves and feathery
plumes of beige to pink flowers on upright stalks are both deer resistant
and low maintenance. Simply cut the plants down to 6 inches in the early
spring. No other care is necessary.

CHALLENGE #4: A COLORLESS GARDEN WITH NO PIZZAZZ

If you ask a homeowner what trait they value the most in their garden, they're likely to give a hearty nod to color. Colorful flowers are the mainstay of most gardens, and smart gardeners aim to have a few different plants in bloom from early spring all the way through fall's first frost (and beyond if you live in a warmer climate). However, you'd be wise to remember that color doesn't always equate to blooms. While a flowering perennial or shrub may be in bloom for only a few short weeks, vivid plant foliage can provide months of color. One of the easiest ways to pump up the volume of a garden is to incorporate a few different foliage colors into the mix. There are dozens of plants with foliage that's chartreuse, pink, burgundy, white, purple, yellow, bronze, rust, red, orange, and everything in between. Don't be afraid to use a few of these plants to add more color your landscape.

Whether you're adding color through flowers, foliage, or a combination of both, here are some bold and beautiful compact plants with an endless supply of pizzazz to perk up even the dullest landscape. Some are meant to offer season-long foliage color, while others lend a bright hue through their blooms.

Compact plants to add brightness to a drab garden

1. POPROCKS™ RAINBOW FIZZ™ SPIREA (*SPIREA JAPONICA* 'MATGOLD'): This super fun flowering shrub has compact foliage that's copper colored in the spring and then matures to a bright yellow-green with red tips. In spring and early summer, the branch tips host flat-topped, inch-wide clusters of bright pink flowers. Due to their fuzzy appearance, the flower clusters look like little fizzy pink clouds. With the ability to handle temperatures down to −40°F, Rainbow Fizz™ is 3 to 4 feet tall and wide at maturity.

2. JAZZ HANDS® VARIEGATED CHINESE FRINGE-FLOWER (*LOROPETALUM CHINENSE* 'IRODORI'): Prized for its unique-colored foliage, this shrub is among the most striking compact plants you can add to your landscape. Winter hardy down to 0°F, the leaves of this variegated Chinese fringe-flower are white and pink upon emergence in the spring, but they mature to a rich, dark purple. Pink, fringe-like flowers occur on stem tips in the mid-spring. A height of 4 to 6 feet with a 4-foot spread means this shrub stays naturally pint sized, but if you want to keep it even smaller, a quick trim just after the blooms fade will do the trick.

3. WINECRAFT BLACK® SMOKE BUSH (*COTINUS COGGYGRIA* 'NCC01'): The misty, smoke-like bloom clusters of smoke bush have been a favorite of gardeners for generations, but most cultivars grow way too large for urban gardens.

Winecraft Black®, however, tops out at just 4 to 6 feet tall and wide. The merlot-colored leaves turn near black in the summer and develop an orange/red hue in the fall. Winter hardy down to −30°F, this smoke bush has a naturally rounded habit.

4. RAZZLE DAZZLE® DWARF CRAPE MYRTLE (*LAGERSTROEMIA* 'GAMAD VI'): Crape myrtles are the darlings of almost every gardener south of the Mason-Dixon Line. While crape myrtle trees are stunning, they outgrow the confines of a smaller garden in short order. Instead, those with limited space should turn to dwarf cultivars like this one instead. Mildew resistant and reaching just 3 to 4 feet tall and wide, Razzle Dazzle® features large heads of hot pink/purple blooms in early summer. Winter hardy down to −10°F, it's an excellent choice for mass plantings. If you garden in a colder climate, opt for growing it in a container that can be overwintered in a garage.

5. SIZZLE & SPICE™ THREADLEAF COREOPSIS SERIES (*COREOPSIS VERTICILLATA* CULTIVARS): This series of dwarf coreopsis are known for their compact growth habit and prolific blooms. The Sizzle & Spice™ series is host to several different varieties that come in shades of pink, yellow, orange, and red, among several bi-colors. Maxing out at just 1 to 1½ feet tall and surviving winters as low as −20°F, the daisy-like blooms are produced in abundance in early summer and should be sheared off when spent to generate another flush of blooms.

6. ARIZONA SUN BLANKET FLOWER (GAILLARDIA × *GRANDIFLORA* 'ARIZONA SUN'): Gorgeous, 2-inch-wide flowers with red petals edged in yellow and red centers grace this plant every summer in droves. Forming a tidy mound of lance-shaped foliage, 'Arizona Sun' is an excellent pollinator plant that stands 12 inches tall and 15 inches wide. Though it dislikes wet, clay-based soils, the plant easily survives winters down to −40°F and brings tons of bold color to the garden.

7. DWARF GOLDENROD (*SOLIDAGO SPHACELATA* 'GOLDEN FLEECE'): If a late-season pop of color is a need for your garden, this plant delivers. An easy-to-grow cultivar of a favorite North American native plant, 'Golden Fleece' dwarf goldenrod does not spread like crazy, unlike some other goldenrods do. Sprays of tiny yellow flowers grace the 12-inch-tall plants in the early fall. This plant is an important nectar source for bees and butterflies, and with a hardiness down to −30°F, it's a welcome addition to almost every garden.

8. MARCUS FLOWERING SAGE (*SALVIA NEMOROSA* 'MARCUS'): Winter hardy down to −30°F and standing just 6 inches tall and 10 inches wide, this micro salvia is packed with flair. Purple spires of flowers top the plants in the late summer and fall, and the pollinators absolutely adore them. Deer resistance, drought tolerance, and a clump-forming habit add to the list of this plant's many attributes. An exceptionally colorful plant, if you shear Marcus's spent blooms off, another flush of blooms occurs soon after.

CHALLENGE #5: TOO MUCH SHADE

A classic example of "the grass is always greener on the other side," I often find that gardeners with lots of shade are constantly wishing they had more sun. But, there are so many wonderful plants that thrive in the shade; it's time to embrace those dark, shadowy corners of the garden and appreciate them for what they are.

Plants adapted to woodland environments and understory edges are perfect fits for these areas. The good news is that so many of these types of plants are naturally petite, so there isn't always a need to seek out specific compact varieties. But if you're looking for pint-sized versions of some favorite shade plants, here are a handful that I covet.

Compact plants to jazz up shady areas

1. INVINCIBELLE MINI MAUVETTE® HYDRANGEA (*HYDRANGEA ARBORESCENS* 'NCHA7'): A neat little cultivar of our North American native smooth hydrangea, Mini Mauvette® grows just 2 to 3 feet tall and wide. The ball-shaped flower clusters occur on new wood, so there's no way you can prune this shrub incorrectly, as long as you do it in the spring. The strong stems mean the massive mauve-pink blooms are held upright without staking. This lovely hydrangea prefers a touch of morning sun and survives winters down to −40°F.

2. LAVALAMP™ FLARE™ PANICLE HYDRANGEA (*HYDRANGEA PANICULATA* 'KOLMAVESU'): Another adaptable and petite hydrangea that's winter hardy down to −40°F, Lavalamp™ Flare™ produces big, conical flower clusters that are white and age to a brilliant pink. Each upright flower panicle can grow up to 16 inches long! With a mature height of just 2 to 3 feet, that means over half of the plant's height is flowers! Perfect for tiny backyards and containers with limited sun.

3. COMPACT BLUE HOSTA (*HOSTA* 'HALCYON'): Yes, there are a million different hostas out there, and yes, there are many dwarf and miniature varieties, but this old standby is one of my personal favorites. Thick, paddle-shaped, blue leaves and a slow growth rate to a height of 18 inches combine to make this a choice variety for small yards. Winter hardy down to −40°F, 'Halcyon' holds its blue color even in summer's heat. A few other mini hostas worth seeking out are 'Appletini', 'Bitsy Gold', 'Dew Drop', and 'Blue Elf'.

4. DWARF CHINESE ASTILBE (*ASTILBE CHINENSIS* VAR. PUMILA): This sweet little astilbe is far from a new variety, but it sure is a stellar one. Spikes of pinky-purple blooms stand rigid above green, ground-hugging leaves. Often used as a groundcover when densely planted, this low-growing variety thrives in the

shade but can handle some sun, too. The bloom spikes reach 10 inches tall, and, with time, the plants will spread several feet wide. Winter hardy down to −30°F, this deer-resistant, pollinator-friendly plant is a must for adding a punch of color to shady gardens.

5. ASTILBE 'LOOK AT ME' (*ASTILBE × ARENDSII* 'LOOK AT ME'): 'Look at Me' is a dwarf astilbe that has definitely earned its name. In bloom from early to midsummer and winter hardy down to −40°F, the cotton candy pink, wispy flower spikes occur on red stems that stand 18 inches above the low foliage. Small in stature but big on impact, moist soils and shady spots are best for this variety.

6. RED PYGMY® DOGWOOD (*CORNUS FLORIDA* 'RUTNUT'): For those seeking a small flowering tree that thrives under the shade of larger trees, your search is over. This tiny version of the American flowering dogwood produces full-sized, deep pink to red blooms in the spring. The foliage is disease resistant and turns a rusty red in the fall. Red Pygmy® grows to just 8 feet in height with a 6-foot spread, but its slow growth rate means it will take up to 10 years to reach maturity. This petite and truly lovely tree from Rutgers University's breeding program is winter hardy down to −20°F. Another alternative is 'Rosy Teacups' American dogwood.

7. COMPACT GOLD-EDGED TOAD LILY (*TRICYRTIS FORMOSANA* 'GILT EDGE'): In full and glorious bloom from August to September, this compact toad lily produces white, orchid-like blooms with purple speckles in branched clusters at the stem ends and upper leaf axils. The broad leaves are shiny and green with a creamy-white to chartreuse edge. Topping out at just 18 inches tall with a spread of up to 24 inches, this perennial spreads naturally but does not become invasive and survives winters down to −20°F.

8. LITTLE LANTERNS COLUMBINE (*AQUILEGIA CANADENSIS* 'LITTLE LANTERNS'):
A miniature selection of our North American native columbine, the nodding, bright red and yellow flowers occur in late spring. The nectar-filled spurs on the back of the flowers are a favorite of hummingbirds returning from their overwintering sites. Winter hardy down to −40°F, 'Little Lanterns' reaches just 10 inches tall and thrives in full to partial shade. Long-blooming for a columbine (up to a month!), this variety also self-sows quite nicely, increasing the colony slowly over time.

CHALLENGE #6: MINIMAL TEXTURE IN THE LANDSCAPE

The next time you visit a botanical garden or head out on a garden tour and see a garden that really appeals to you, step back and examine the plantings and think about what makes them so effective. In many cases, you'll find that the most interesting plant combinations aren't the result of big, blousy blooms or colorful foliage. Instead, it's the combination of various plant textures that really catches the eye. The strappy, upright, sword-like foliage of one plant combined with the soft, wispy texture of another often yields far more interest than two brightly colored flowers planted side by side ever could. Bringing a diversity of plant textures to the landscape is a must for ensuring there's season-long interest in a garden.

Here are some excellent plants to add more texture to a garden. You can use them as your "texture echo" or just pop them in between existing plants to add more interest wherever it's needed.

Compact plants to add more texture to the garden

1. MAGICAL® SNOW DROPS PEARL BUSH (*EXOCHORDA* 'SNOW DROPS'): This beautiful little deciduous shrub hits just 3 to 4 feet tall and equally as wide. Its compact form makes it perfect for small garden areas. Clusters of delicate white flowers emerge from round, pearl-like buds late in the spring, followed by yellow autumn color late in the season. Winter hardy down to −30°F and loving conditions from full sun to part shade, this compact pearl bush blooms for 3 to 4 weeks every spring. Its soft, graceful texture looks beautiful in shrub beds and flower borders.

2. *CHAMAECYPARIS LAWSONIANA* 'WISSEL'S SAGUARO': A slow-growing tree unlike anything else you've ever seen, this funky plant is straight out of a Dr. Seuss book! The upright branches look a bit like a saguaro cactus, hence the cultivar's name. This unique false cypress is evergreen and reaches a height of about 10 feet with a spread of just 6 to 8 feet. In my opinion, it's the most unique of all the trees for small gardens. It's winter hardy down to −30°F.

3. BANANA BOAT BROAD-LEAVED SEDGE (*CAREX SIDEROSTICHA* 'BANANA BOAT'): Sedges are great choices for full to part shade, but this cultivar grows to just 10 inches tall and wide. Deer resistant and tolerant of moist soils, the bright yellow and green variegate foliage of this grass-like plant gracefully bow across the garden, adding a soft texture that's totally touchable. With an almost bamboo-like appearance, 'Banana Boat' is excellent for edging shady beds and adding brightness to containers, too. The foliage dies back in the winter, but the plants readily survive down to −20°F.

4. DWARF HINOKI CYPRESS (*CHAMAECYPARIS OBTUSA* 'NANA GRACILIS'):

A compact, extremely slow-growing, soft-needled evergreen with a somewhat pyramidal form, dwarf Hinoki cypress have fan-shaped foliage that's lush and dark green and gives the plant an almost feathery texture. Winter hardy down to −30°F and reaching 3 to 5 feet tall and 2 to 3 feet wide over the course of many years, this evergreen requires full to partial sun and well-drained soils.

5. DWARF PINK SPEEDWELL (*VERONICA SPICATA* 'GILES VAN HEES'):

Spikes of bright pink appear in midsummer above the dark green upright foliage of this neat and tidy perennial. A compact cultivar that reaches only 6 inches tall with a 10-inch spread, 'Giles Van Hees' requires full sun. Its spiky texture is a great counterpoint to plants with soft, billowy flowers. Slow spreading and winter hardy down to −40°F, the blooms attract pollinators, too.

6. BLUE DENIM DWARF BEARDED IRIS (*IRIS PUMILA* 'BLUE DENIM'):

'Blue Denim' is a spring bloomer whose sword-like foliage adds great texture to perennial borders and beds, even when the plants aren't in bloom. Mature at 12 to 18 inches tall, this iris produces early-spring blooms and is winter hardy down to −30°F. The flowers are ruffled and denim blue, and it blooms several weeks earlier than taller varieties. This miniature perennial should be planted with the top of the thick root (rhizome) sticking out above the soil.

7. DWARF JOE-PYE WEED (*EUPATORIUM DUBIUM* 'LITTLE JOE' [SYN. *EUTROCHIUM DUBIUM* 'LITTLE JOE']):

Fuzzy clusters of mauve blooms top the stiff, upright stems of this compact perennial in late summer. At one-third to one-half the height of traditional Joe-pye weed, 'Little Joe' is a bee and butterfly magnet. A cultivar of a North American native plant that thrives in average to wet garden soils, it maxes out at just 3 to 4 feet tall and 1 to 3 feet wide, so no staking is required. The blooms add an airy texture to the garden late in the season, and the plants are winter hardy down to −40°F.

8. TWOMBLY'S RED SENTINEL JAPANESE MAPLE (*ACER PALMATUM* 'TWOMBLY'S RED SENTINEL'):

Though most Japanese maples are wide spreading, this cultivar boasts very upright growth, making it one of the best trees for small gardens and tight spaces. The foliage is a striking, deep red in spring and summer; even the stems are red. 'Twombly's Red Sentinel' maxes out at 15 feet in height and spreads just 6 feet wide. Winter hardy down to −20°F, the palm-shaped leaves of this deciduous tree lighten to a bright crimson red in the autumn. Its slow growth rate means this variety will take many years to reach maturity.

CHALLENGE #7: LACK OF EVERGREEN PLANTS FOR YEAR-ROUND INTEREST

Evergreen plants have much to offer. Not only do they provide four seasons of visual interest to the garden; they also serve as windbreaks, increase privacy, and provide food and shelter for birds and other wildlife. Unfortunately, most home landscapes include the same five or six evergreens, most of which grow way too large for smaller gardens. The constant pruning these plants require makes them high maintenance and labor intensive. Why fuss with full-sized evergreens like yews, arborvitaes, spruces, and rhododendrons that reach all the way up to the eaves of your house when the following compact evergreen shrubs provide all the benefits of the "big guys" but in a much more manageable package?

Compact plants that are evergreen

1. COMPACT MAXIMUM RHODODENDRON (*RHODODENDRON* 'MAXIMUM COMPACTA'):
A mini version of a traditional rhododendron, this broad-leaved evergreen produces large clusters of pinkish lavender flowers in late spring. A low-growing, bushy plant, it makes a great addition to foundation plantings and shrub borders that receive full to partial sun. Reaching just 3 feet tall and wide, bumblebees love the flowers and are often found buzzing around the blooms. With winter hardiness down to −40°F, there's no pruning necessary to maintain the shrub's natural shape and size. Another compact rhododendron worth seeking out is the purple-flowered 'Ramapo'.

2. COMPACT INKBERRY HOLLY (*ILEX GLABRA* 'COMPACTA'):
Another dwarf evergreen, this shrub is densely branched with elongated, oval leaves that are a dark, glossy green. This variety is female and will also produce small, dark berries that persist on the plant through winter if a pollinating male variety is nearby. It's fairly deer resistant, too, making it a good choice for deer-plagued landscapes. Winter hardy down to −30°F, compact inkberry makes an excellent hedge or foundation plant. With a thick, twiggy habit that tops out at 4 to 6 feet in height and spread, it can also be regularly pruned to be kept even smaller.

3. DWARF JAPANESE BLACK PINE (*PINUS THUNBERGII* 'KOTOBUKI'):
Fully winter hardy down to −20°F, this needled evergreen reaches just 4 feet tall and 2 feet wide. The upright candles of new growth in the spring, coupled with its narrow growth habit, make this an excellent choice for containers and small gardens. Slow growing, with a dense structure, this deer-resistant evergreen has needles that are about half the length of regular Japanese black pines.

4. DWARF PENCIL POINT JUNIPER (*JUNIPERUS COMMUNIS* 'COMPRESSA'):
Evergreen and columnar in form, dwarf pencil point juniper is both unique and slow growing. With an average height of 5 feet and a width of

just 1 foot, this sun-loving evergreen has blue-green needles. Female plants may produce blue "berries" in the fall, as well. Its tapered form means it's a great "exclamation point" accent plant for smaller landscapes. Winter hardy down to −40°F.

5. DWARF JAPANESE HOLLY (*ILEX CRENATA* 'DWARF PAGODA'): This is such a great little plant! Reaching just 3 feet tall and 1 to 2 feet wide at maturity, miniature Japanese holly is super slow growing (it grows only about an inch a year!) and winter hardy down to −20°F. Preferring full sun to light shade, the tiny, round, evergreen leaves are glossy and dark green; and they're stacked against each other in rows along the stems, giving the plant a really interesting appearance. Introduced through Rutgers University, this selection looks like a funky bonsai plant and is excellent for rock gardens and patio beds.

6. UPRIGHT JAPANESE PLUM YEW (*CEPHALOXATUS HARRINGTONIA* 'FASTIGIATA'):
This broad-needled evergreen is winter hardy down to −10°F. Its upright, slender growth habit maxes out at 8 feet tall and 3 feet wide. Though it's nonflowering, Japanese plum yews have dark green needles that are densely spaced on bottlebrush-like, upright branches. Each needle is about 2 inches long. It thrives in full to partial sun but prefers afternoon shade in hot southern regions during the summer months.

7. COMPACT OREGON HOLLY GRAPE (*MAHONIA AQUIFOLIUM* 'COMPACTA'): Oregon holly grapes are attention-grabbing plants, and this compact selection is no different. The new growth is bronze colored, and it ages to a deep, glossy green. Then in fall, the foliage turns a rich purple-red. The fragrant yellow flowers in spring are followed by elongated clusters of purple, grape-like fruits in the summer and fall. With a low and spreading growth habit, compact Oregon holly grape adapts well to shadier spots, but be forewarned that the edges of the leaves have sharp spines. Useful as a low hedge or underplanting, this selection matures at 2 to 3 feet tall and 3 to 4 feet wide, and is winter hardy down to −20°F.

8. LITTLE GIANT DWARF ARBORVITAE (*THUJA OCCIDENTALIS* 'LITTLE GIANT'): Most people think of arborvitae as being tall and cone shaped, but this compact variety is globe shaped, reaching just 4 feet tall and wide. Winter hardy down to −40°F, this slow-growing, rounded shrub produces soft, feathery, fan-shaped foliage. Its tidy shape needs no pruning, making it a terrific choice for foundation plantings, low hedges, or along garden edges.

CHALLENGE #8: NOT ENOUGH POLLINATORS

Gardens can be really beautiful places, full of color and interest, that bring peace and joy to those who tend and visit them. But, gardens also serve purposes far beyond their beauty. Gardens foster and support pollinators and other insects, increase local biodiversity, and provide food and shelter for many species of mammals, amphibians, reptiles, and birds. Selecting plants and planning a garden that benefits nonhuman creatures, too, is of increasing importance as natural habitats disappear.

Whether you want to provide nectar and habitat for pollinators simply to improve your garden's biodiversity or you're aiming to increase pollination for your edibles, here are some of the best compact plants to attract and support a broad diversity of pollinating insects.

Compact plants to attract pollinators

1. MAGICAL® MOONLIGHT BUTTONBUSH (*CEPHALANTHUS OCCIDENTALIS* 'MOONLIGHT'): A compact version of a North American native shrub, Magical® Moonlight buttonbush is an exceptional pollinator plant. It lures and supports bees, hummingbirds, and butterflies while in bloom. Standing at half the height and width of the straight species, this cultivar matures at just 5 to 8 feet tall and 4 to 6 feet wide. A very adaptable shrub that produces golf ball–sized, creamy-white, round flower clusters in late spring, buttonbush thrives in full sun to part shade and is winter hardy down to −20°F. Pollinators pack the bloom clusters for their pollen and nectar. Great for bogs and poorly drained sites, buttonbush also performs like a champ in regular garden soils, too.

2. LITTLE HENRY® VIRGINIA SWEETSPIRE (*ITEA VIRGINICA* 'LITTLE HENRY'): A longtime favorite of mine, this small-statured Virginia sweetspire is covered with pendulous clusters of fragrant, white flowers in the spring. In the fall, the thick, medium green foliage turns a brilliant red. This is a cultivar of a North American native shrub that the pollinators absolutely adore. It maxes out at about 2 to 3 feet tall and wide and is winter hardy down to −20°F.

3. SAPPHIRE SURF™ BLUEBEARD (*CARYOPTERIS × CLANDONENSIS* 'BLAUER SPLATZ'): A low-maintenance, mounding shrub with deep blue blooms that will knock your socks off, this compact version of the blue mist shrub is all that and a bag of chips. Reaching just 2 feet tall and 3 feet wide, this deer-resistant shrub is smothered in flat-topped, fuzzy flower clusters in late summer through fall. The blooms are covered with a variety of bee species every day, from sunrise to sunset. Requiring full sun and winter hardy down to −20°F, Sapphire Surf's only care requirement is an early spring haircut, when its woody stems should be cut down to about 8 to 10 inches in height.

4. BUTTERFLY™ JULIA CONEFLOWER (*ECHINACEA* 'JULIA'): Coneflowers are
the darlings of perennial gardeners everywhere. But, urban gardeners
with limited space may find they take up far too much room. Enter
Butterfly™ Julia coneflower. Reaching just 15 inches tall, this selection
is sturdy, compact, strong, and floriferous. Tangerine-colored, 4-inch-
wide flowers are produced from midsummer through early fall. Single-
petaled coneflowers like this one are generally better for pollinators than
double-flowered types, as their nectaries are more accessible. Shrugging
off winters down to −30°F, coneflowers require full sun; and they make a
great cut flower, too.

5. PURPLE DOME NEW ENGLAND ASTER (*SYMPHYOTRICHUM NOVAE-ANGLIAE* 'PURPLE DOME'): If you're looking for late-season color in an itty-bitty
perennial package, 'Purple Dome' aster has you covered. With its mounding
form and bushy growth habit, this cultivar of a North American native plant
blooms in early fall with hundreds of deep purple, ½-inch-wide blooms
graced with yellow centers. The entire plant is covered in color when this
variety is in bloom. An excellent late-season nectar source for pollinators
that's winter hardy down to −30°F, 'Purple Dome' reaches just 12 to 18
inches tall and 3 feet wide with no staking required.

6. PARDON MY PURPLE DWARF BEE BALM (*MONARDA DIDYMA* 'PARDON MY PURPLE'): A summer-blooming perennial that's winter hardy down to
−30°F, this compact bee balm requires little more than full sun and average
garden soil. In bloom for weeks at a time, it maxes out at just 10 to 12
inches tall, making it the perfect choice for small-scale pollinator gardens.
A cultivar of a North American native plant, 'Pardon My Purple' is a pint-
sized version of a garden favorite. The flowers are deep fuchsia purple, and
both the flowers and the deer- and powdery mildew-resistant foliage are
edible and make a wonderful herbal tea when dried. This variety is one
of several selections in the Pardon My series of compact monardas. Other
varieties produce light pink, lavender, and cerise blooms.

7. BLACK ADDER ANISE HYSSOP (*AGASTACHE RUGOSUM × A. FOENICULUM* 'BLACK ADDER'): The slender, bottlebrush-shaped, bright blue flower clusters of
'Black Adder' hyssop are a favorite of many species of bees. In bloom from
midsummer until frost, this licorice-scented plant looks great in containers
and garden beds. With a mature height and width of 2 to 3 feet and a
winter hardiness of −10°F, 'Black Adder' forms an upright clump that's a
good foot shorter than other varieties of this perennial. And as an added
bonus, anise hyssop is deer, drought, and heat resistant, too.

5

MORE COMPACT PLANTS FOR THE YARD AND LANDSCAPE:
40 Profiles

In this chapter, let's take a deep dive into the world of compact plants by viewing detailed profiles of 40 more exceptional plants for small spaces. They're divided into three distinct categories based on their growth habit: shrubs, trees, and perennials. Edible plants, including herbs, vegetables, and fruits, are featured in the next chapter. Each plant profile found here includes specifics on the appearance and hardiness of the highlighted plant, along with details about its mature dimensions and preferred growing conditions. You'll also find a special section for each plant that features additional useful information to help ensure your success.

Keep in mind, though, that this is a collection of basic growing information for these plants, but the performance of each variety is also based on the precise growing conditions of your climate and how well you take care of whatever you plant. Gardeners in northern climates are likely to have different results than those growing in warm southern areas. And those who pay careful attention to the needs of each plant in terms of its care and maintenance are sure to see better results than those who completely ignore the garden soon after it's planted. The maintenance tips offered in chapter 2 will help ensure your success, no matter which compact plants you decide to include in your garden.

Let's get rolling and meet more of my favorite compact plants.

Firefly™ Nightglow™ Diervilla

COMMON NAME: Firefly™ Nightglow™ Diervilla

BOTANICAL NAME: *Diervilla splendens* 'El Madrigal'

PLANT TYPE: Flowering shrub; deciduous

MATURE DIMENSIONS: 2 to 3 feet tall and equally as wide

HARDINESS: Winter hardy down to −30°F (USDA Zones 4–8)

IDEAL SUN CONDITIONS: Full sun

PHYSICAL APPEARANCE: Bright yellow, trumpet-like flowers, combined with dark red foliage, make this dwarf red-leaved bush honeysuckle a real standout. Clusters of blooms top the branches from early summer through fall, with peak bloom occurring in midsummer, when hummingbirds and other pollinators visit this small shrub in droves. In autumn, the burgundy-red foliage color deepens even more.

CARE REQUIREMENTS: Firefly™ Nightglow™ Diervilla thrives in well-drained soil that's slightly acidic. It has low water requirements once it's established but needs to be regularly irrigated for the first year or two. After that, this sporty little shrub tolerates both drought and heat.

EXTRA INFO: Because of its pollinator appeal, this compact Diervilla makes a great addition to a small-scale pollinator garden. It's a terrific edging plant, too, adding curb appeal to sidewalk beds and foundation plantings.

Sugartina® Crystalina Clethra

COMMON NAME: Sugartina® Crystalina Clethra

BOTANICAL NAME: *Clethra alnifolia* 'Crystalina'

PLANT TYPE: Flowering shrub; deciduous

MATURE DIMENSIONS: 2 to 3 feet tall; equal width

HARDINESS: Winter hardy down to −30°F (USDA Zones 4–9)

IDEAL SUN CONDITIONS: Partial to full sun

PHYSICAL APPEARANCE: Summersweet has long been a personal favorite of mine for both its form and its flowers. This compact variety is extra sensational because it fits in tight quarters without complaint. The fragrant, creamy-white, oval flower puffs appear in midsummer, luring in butterflies and other pollinators. Oval green leaves turn a striking yellow color in autumn, and its natural mounding habit means it's suitable to many different garden environments.

CARE REQUIREMENTS: Clethra, in general, requires minimal maintenance, but Sugartina® Crystalina is even more carefree, since little, if any, pruning is required. If you must prune to remove dead growth or limit its size even further, early spring is the best time to do so. It thrives in average garden soil and even tolerates damp areas without missing a beat.

EXTRA INFO: This is a compact cultivar of a North American native plant. It's deer resistant, and the sweet fragrance of the flowers is always a nice surprise when the plant first comes into flower.

Bobo® Panicle Hydrangea

COMMON NAME: Bobo® Panicle Hydrangea

BOTANICAL NAME: *Hydrangea paniculata* 'ILVOBO'

PLANT TYPE: Flowering shrub; deciduous

MATURE DIMENSIONS: 2 to 3 feet tall; 3 to 4 feet wide

HARDINESS: Winter hardy down to −40°F (USDA Zones 3–8)

IDEAL SUN CONDITIONS: Full to partial sun

PHYSICAL APPEARANCE: A spectacular dwarf hydrangea that bears full-size blooms on an itty-bitty plant. Large, white, conical panicles of flowers occur in summer on strong, upright stems that do not require staking. This prolific bloomer is in flower for months; the blooms progress to pink as they age, and they dry beautifully. Bobo's mounding habit and lush green foliage mean it's beautiful in the spring, too, even before the plant comes into flower.

CARE REQUIREMENTS: A compact hydrangea that tolerates average garden soil, Bobo® also performs well in containers, though it will wilt if not regularly watered. A member of the paniculata group, this variety blooms on new wood, so pruning in the early spring will not affect the flower production for the coming season like it does for some other types of hydrangeas. You can even prune Bobo® all the way down to the ground in March and it will be in full bloom just a few months later.

EXTRA INFO: There's another lovely petite hydrangea called Little Lime™ that grows a bit taller than Bobo® but is equally as winter hardy. Its flowers are a striking lime green that ages to a soft pink.

Lil' Ditty® Witherod Viburnum

COMMON NAME: Lil' Ditty® Witherod Viburnum

BOTANICAL NAME: *Viburnum cassinoides* 'SMNVCDD'

PLANT TYPE: Flowering shrub; deciduous

MATURE DIMENSIONS: 1 to 2 feet tall; 2 to 3 feet wide

HARDINESS: Winter hardy down to −40°F (USDA Zones 3–8)

IDEAL SUN CONDITIONS: Full to partial sun

PHYSICAL APPEARANCE: This is among the most beautiful space-saving plants available to home gardeners. It's prized for multiple seasons of interest. Puff balls of creamy-white, fragrant flowers occur every spring atop bright green foliage. The flowers are very long lasting and are borne prolifically on this compact, mounding shrub. Soon after bloom, the plant produces round berries that start green, then progress to pink, red, and eventually near-black, and persist on the plant well into winter (or whenever the songbirds find them!). The presence of two or more plants improves pollination and fruit set.

CARE REQUIREMENTS: Like most viburnums, this variety is adaptable to a wide range of growing conditions and soils. It blooms on old wood, so any pruning should occur immediately after flowering, though pruning is seldom required at all. Moist but well-drained soils are best. Lil' Ditty® is tolerant of moderately wet areas, too.

EXTRA INFO: Lil' Ditty® is a dwarf cultivar of a North American native plant. It's deer resistant and very adaptable, making it perfect for foundation plantings, shrub borders, and perennial garden accents.

My Monet® Weigela

COMMON NAME: My Monet® Weigela

BOTANICAL NAME: *Weigela florida* 'Verweig'

PLANT TYPE: Flowering shrub; deciduous

MATURE DIMENSIONS: 12 to 18 inches tall; 2 feet wide

HARDINESS: Winter hardy down to −30°F (USDA Zones 4–6)

IDEAL SUN CONDITIONS: Full to partial sun

PHYSICAL APPEARANCE: This colorful little shrub definitely deserves to have Monet's name included in its own. The foliage is green with a creamy-white variegated edge that turns pink in full-sun conditions. Every spring, the stems are loaded with pink trumpet-like blooms that are long lasting and adored by various pollinators, including hummingbirds and butterflies. If the plant is happy, you'll occasionally see sporadic fall flowering as well.

CARE REQUIREMENTS: The tight growth habit of My Monet® means it needs no pruning. It's deer resistant but won't tolerate waterlogged soils. Weigela's don't perform well in hot climates, so avoid planting them in southern regions.

EXTRA INFO: This sweet shrub makes quite a statement in a mass planting around a patio's edge or in containers on a sunny balcony or deck.

Lil' Kim® Rose-of-Sharon

COMMON NAME: Lil' Kim® Rose-of-Sharon

BOTANICAL NAME: *Hibiscus syriacus* 'Antong Two'

PLANT TYPE: Flowering shrub; deciduous

MATURE DIMENSIONS: 3 to 4 feet tall; equal spread

HARDINESS: Winter hardy down to −20°F (USDA Zones 5–9)

IDEAL SUN CONDITIONS: Full sun

PHYSICAL APPEARANCE: Half the size of a regular rose-of-Sharon, Lil' Kim® produces dozens of flowers on each and every stem. Blooms are 3 inches wide and white with a central red-pink marking on each petal. And, to sweeten the deal even more, it's in bloom all summer long! The upright growth habit keeps the blooms unspoiled and makes Lil' Kim® a great choice for containers.

CARE REQUIREMENTS: Like other rose-of-Sharon bushes, this compact variety is very forgiving of lousy soil, heat tolerant, drought tolerant, and salt tolerant. Though pruning is seldom needed, this shrub blooms on new wood, so pruning should always occur in the early spring.

EXTRA INFO: Lil' Kim® is so easygoing that it's said to bloom beautifully even in its first year. Blooms are attractive to bees and butterflies, and the plants are deer resistant.

Elsdancer Tiny Dancer™ Lilac

COMMON NAME: Elsdancer Tiny Dancer™ Lilac

BOTANICAL NAME: *Syringa vulgaris* 'Elsdancer'

PLANT TYPE: Flowering shrub; deciduous

MATURE DIMENSIONS: 4 to 5 feet tall; 3 to 4 feet wide

HARDINESS: Winter hardy down to −30°F (USDA Zones 4–8)

IDEAL SUN CONDITIONS: Full to partial sun

PHYSICAL APPEARANCE: Few things rival the fragrance of a spring lilac bloom. This compact variety produces intensely fragrant, lavender-blue flower clusters in May and June that are 4 to 5 inches long and very full. The large, heart-shaped leaves are a great backdrop for the blooms. This is a great plant for foundations, flower borders, and shrub beds. It also makes an excellent cut flower.

CARE REQUIREMENTS: Tiny Dancer™ lilac prefers moist, but well-drained soil with average fertility. It's remarkably heat tolerant. Requiring minimum care, this dwarf lilac blooms on old wood, so prune only after flowering.

EXTRA INFO: As an added bonus, this lilac is both powdery mildew resistant and heat tolerant, making it a good choice for southern regions where most lilacs won't grow well.

Sugar Plum Fairy® Lilac

COMMON NAME: Sugar Plum Fairy® Lilac

BOTANICAL NAME: *Syringa vulgaris* 'Bailsugar'

PLANT TYPE: Flowering shrub; deciduous

MATURE DIMENSIONS: 4 feet tall and 5 feet wide

HARDINESS: Winter hardy down to −40°F (USDA Zones 3–8)

IDEAL SUN CONDITIONS: Full to partial sun

PHYSICAL APPEARANCE: Smothered in frothy, rosy-pink flowers in late spring through early summer, Sugar Plum Fairy® not only looks good in foundation and flower beds, but it also makes a stunning hedge. The spicy, sweet fragrance of the blooms lures in hummingbirds, butterflies, and other pollinators. This lilac's leaf shade is medium green, and its growth habit is a loose mound.

CARE REQUIREMENTS: Plan to irrigate this compact shrub during dry periods, but other than that, it's fairly bulletproof. Avoid planting in waterlogged areas, as it can lead to root rot. Prune immediately after flowering, if any pruning is required at all. Disease resistant.

EXTRA INFO: Sugar Plum Fairy® is one in a series of lilacs known as the Fairytale series. This is the smallest-statured one.

Little Devil™ Ninebark

COMMON NAME: Little Devil™ Ninebark

BOTANICAL NAME: *Physocarpus opulifolius* 'Donna May'

PLANT TYPE: Flowering shrub; deciduous

MATURE DIMENSIONS: 3 to 4 feet tall; 3 to 4 feet wide

HARDINESS: Winter hardy down to −40°F (USDA Zones 3–7)

IDEAL SUN CONDITIONS: Full to partial sun

PHYSICAL APPEARANCE: The upright, arching habit of this native woody plant looks spectacular in shrub beds, flower borders, and front-walk plantings. Half the height of a regular ninebark, Little Devil™ has fine-textured foliage that's dark burgundy. In June, clusters of small, pale pink blooms occur along the branches and make a striking display when combined with the foliage. A smattering of smaller blooms occur off and on throughout the growing season. In fall, small red berries develop. This is a compact shrub that's very well branched.

CARE REQUIREMENTS: This dwarf ninebark resists powdery mildew and is tolerant of both wet and dry soil conditions. It's very easy to care for, though if you must prune, be sure to do so just after the blooms fade.

EXTRA INFO: Native to the eastern half of the United States and up into Canada, ninebark is a very adaptable shrub. This compact cultivar makes a great low hedgerow plant for supporting pollinators and other beneficial insects.

Little Mischief Rose

COMMON NAME: Little Mischief Rose

BOTANICAL NAME: *Rosa* 'BAlief'

PLANT TYPE: Flowering woody ornamental

MATURE DIMENSIONS: 2 to 3 feet tall; 2 to 4 feet wide

HARDINESS: Winter hardy down to −30°F (USDA Zones 4–9)

IDEAL SUN CONDITIONS: Full sun

PHYSICAL APPEARANCE: If you're looking for a little rose to mix into your perennial beds or foundation plantings, Little Mischief is it! This compact rose produces clusters of fragrant, cerise-pink blooms that age to a soft pink. Each bloom is double-petaled and 1 inch across. Its repeat blooming habit means it's in constant flower from early summer through fall. The foliage is deep green, shiny, and disease resistant. Not only does this dwarf rose look good in beds, it also works beautifully in drifts or container plantings.

CARE REQUIREMENTS: This compact member of the Easy Elegance® rose series requires very little care. All you have to do is make sure it's well watered for the first two seasons, until the roots become established. Mulch in the spring and deadhead as necessary. No fungicides required.

EXTRA INFO: Unlike many other roses, Little Mischief is not grafted; it's grown on its own root stock, so there are no worries about burying it too deeply and having another rose sprout from the root stock.

Marge Miller™ Camellia

COMMON NAME: Marge Miller™ Camellia

BOTANICAL NAME: *Camellia sasanqua* 'Marge Miller'

PLANT TYPE: Flowering evergreen shrub/groundcover

MATURE DIMENSIONS: 1 foot tall; 3 to 4 feet wide

HARDINESS: Winter hardy down to 0°F (USDA Zones 7–10)

IDEAL SUN CONDITIONS: Partial sun

PHYSICAL APPEARANCE:

A quintessential southern beauty, camellias deserve a place in every home garden, but full-sized camellias are far too big for smaller backyards. This dwarf variety acts more like a groundcover than a shrub. Marge Miller's™ naturally spreading form produces blooms from fall through winter. Plant it at the top of a wall for a shower of cascading, pink, double-petaled blooms that look much like roses. The glossy green foliage is a knockout, too.

CARE REQUIREMENTS: Consistent moisture is key with camellias, so mulch the plants well. This also helps keep roots cool. Use an acid fertilizer after flowering each year to keep the plants in tip-top shape.

EXTRA INFO: This Australian introduction is the first prostrate camellia in the world. It's a spectacular choice for mass plantings in warm climates.

World's Fair Crape Myrtle

COMMON NAME: World's Fair Crape Myrtle

BOTANICAL NAME: *Lagerstroemia indica* 'World's Fair'

PLANT TYPE: Flowering shrub; deciduous

MATURE DIMENSIONS: 2 to 3 feet wide; 3- to 4-foot spread

HARDINESS: Winter hardy down to −10°F (USDA Zones 6–8)

IDEAL SUN CONDITIONS: Full sun

PHYSICAL APPEARANCE: Though this plant grows in a limited climate range, the big clusters of watermelon-pink flowers of this crape myrtle can't be beat. In addition to being a gorgeous addition to flower beds and borders, 'World's Fair' can be used as a groundcover, too. It's in bloom from late spring through early summer, and its dark, glossy leaves look great even when the plant is not in flower.

CARE REQUIREMENTS: Like other crape myrtles, this compact variety prefers mildly acidic soil conditions and is fairly salt tolerant, making it a good choice for seaside gardens. Crape myrtles bloom on new wood so do any necessary pruning in early spring.

EXTRA INFO: 'World's Fair' is attractive to many pollinators.

Shaina Japanese Maple

COMMON NAME: Shaina Japanese Maple

BOTANICAL NAME: *Acer palmatum* 'Shaina'

PLANT TYPE: Tree; deciduous

MATURE DIMENSIONS: 6 to 8 feet tall; 8 to 10 feet wide

HARDINESS: Winter hardy down to −20°F (USDA Zones 5–8)

IDEAL SUN CONDITIONS: Full to partial sun

PHYSICAL APPEARANCE: Though Japanese maples in general are lovely small trees for the landscape, 'Shaina' Japanese maple is extra special. Its compact form and dense branching habit are perfect for pint-sized gardens. The new foliage is bright red in the spring and then matures to a deep wine-red in summer. Its slow growth rate makes it the ideal tree for container culture, too. Shaina is spectacular under the canopy of larger trees, where it develops even better leaf color.

CARE REQUIREMENTS: Like other Japanese maples, 'Shaina' enjoys moist, well-drained soil and requires regular irrigation through dry spells. Acidic soils are best, and be sure to protect this little tree from high winds, especially in the winter. In hot climates, provide shade in the afternoon, as leaf scorch can develop with excessive sun exposure. Little to no pruning is required, though if you must do so, be sure to prune in early winter before the sap starts to run.

EXTRA INFO: This cultivar is an Asian native. Japanese maples are a big family that's been bred into many different beautiful varieties. Other cultivars for small-scale gardens are 'Coonara Pygmy', 'Beni Kawa', 'Murasaki Kiyohime', 'Villa Taranto', 'Inaba Shidare', 'Maiku Jaku', and 'Caperci Dwarf', though most of these grow to twice the height of 'Shaina'.

Regent Serviceberry

COMMON NAME: Regent Serviceberry

BOTANICAL NAME: *Amelanchier alnifolia* 'Regent'

PLANT TYPE: Multistemmed tree; deciduous

MATURE DIMENSIONS: 4 to 6 feet tall; equal spread

HARDINESS: Winter hardy down to −50°F (USDA Zones 2–7)

IDEAL SUN CONDITIONS: Full to partial sun

PHYSICAL APPEARANCE: Serviceberries are one of my favorite landscape trees, and 'Regent' is a serviceberry unlike any other. The only compact serviceberry out there, it's nothing short of stellar. This upright, multi-branched tree produces purplish leaf growth in the spring, followed by numerous ¾-inch-wide, five-petaled, fragrant flowers. The leaves then age to a bluish green with light undersides. Dark blue berries follow soon after. The berries are delicious and perfectly edible, if you can beat the birds to them. Oh, and to sweeten the deal, Regent serviceberry also has a beautiful yellow-orange fall color.

CARE REQUIREMENTS: Serviceberries are tolerant of lousy soils, wet soils, drought, and very cold winters. In other words, they're extremely adaptable. Perform a renewal pruning every few years by removing the oldest stems down to the ground and allowing the younger shoots to develop.

EXTRA INFO: This miniature variety was selected in North Dakota. It is a cultivar of a North American native plant. Pollinators and birds adore it.

Ace of Hearts Eastern Redbud

COMMON NAME: Ace of Hearts Eastern Redbud

BOTANICAL NAME: *Cercis canadensis* 'Ace of Hearts'

PLANT TYPE: Flowering tree; deciduous

MATURE DIMENSIONS: 10 to 12 feet tall; 13 to 15 feet wide

HARDINESS: Winter hardy down to −20°F (USDA Zones 5–9)

IDEAL SUN CONDITIONS: Full to partial sun; full shade in hot climates

PHYSICAL APPEARANCE: Ace of Hearts has all the merits of a full-sized redbud but in a tidy little package. In early spring, expect a powerful burst of tiny, purple-pink blooms held tight to the branches in dense clusters. Soon after bloom, perfectly heart-shaped, green leaves appear, stacked and layered along the branches. The flowers are occasionally followed by flat, bean-like seedpods. This is a cultivar of an eastern North American native tree.

CARE REQUIREMENTS: Redbuds prefer slightly alkaline soil that's moist but well-drained. Be sure to water this little tree regularly until it's established. It's beautiful, naturally dwarf shape means no pruning is necessary.

EXTRA INFO: As if Ace of Hearts weren't already amazing enough, its yellow fall color is icing on the cake. Plus, the flowers are edible and adored by insect pollinators and hummingbirds, alike.

Sargent Tina Crabapple

COMMON NAME: Sargent Tina Crabapple

BOTANICAL NAME: *Malus sargentii* 'Tina'

PLANT TYPE: Flowering tree; deciduous

MATURE DIMENSIONS: 5 feet tall; 6 feet wide

HARDINESS: Winter hardy down to −30°F (USDA Zones 4–8)

IDEAL SUN CONDITIONS: Full sun

PHYSICAL APPEARANCE: Among the smallest crabapples on the market, Sargent Tina is a petite powerhouse. A flush of inch-wide, white flowers bursts from dark pink buds in early spring. The spreading branches and moderate growth rate make Sargent Tina an exceptional urban street tree. The ¼-inch red fruits are adored by birds in the fall and winter.

CARE REQUIREMENTS: Sargent Tina shows improved pest and disease resistance, so there's no need to worry about apple scab and other issues. Select a site with well-drained soil and water the tree regularly until it's established. Any pruning should take place during the winter dormant season. Sargent Tina is typically grafted to create a tree form, so, like other crabapples, don't plant too deeply or it may develop root suckers.

EXTRA INFO: This tough little tree is a cultivar of an Asian species introduced by Charles Sargent of the Arnold Arboretum at Harvard University. It was then bred to produce 'Tina' and several other cultivars.

Apollo® Sugar Maple

COMMON NAME: Apollo® Sugar Maple

BOTANICAL NAME: *Acer saccharum* 'Barrett Cole'

PLANT TYPE: Tree; deciduous

MATURE DIMENSIONS: 20 to 25 feet tall;
8 to 10 feet wide

HARDINESS: Winter hardy down to −30°F (USDA
Zones 4–7)

IDEAL SUN CONDITIONS: Full sun

PHYSICAL APPEARANCE: If you're looking for a
shade tree that won't take over a diminutive
backyard, Apollo® sugar maple might fit the bill.
This narrow, columnar selection of the sugar
maple is very symmetrical. Its extraordinary
yellow-orange to red fall color follows a deep,
luxurious green in the spring and summer.
The compact form and dense branching of this
shapely tree make it ideal for tight spaces and
urban gardens, as long as there's room for it to
grow to its mature height.

CARE REQUIREMENTS: Apollo® is adaptable to
various soils but dislikes compaction. This
tree is naturally quite shapely, so it seldom
needs pruning.

EXTRA INFO: Apollo® sugar maple is a slow-growing
cultivar of a North American native species.

Kikuzaki Dwarf Star Magnolia

COMMON NAME: Kikuzaki Dwarf Star Magnolia

BOTANICAL NAME: *Magnolia kobus* var. *stellata* 'Kikuzaki'

PLANT TYPE: Flowering tree/shrub; deciduous

MATURE DIMENSIONS: 8 to 10 feet tall; 6 to 8 feet wide

HARDINESS: Winter hardy down to −30°F (USDA Zones 4–8)

IDEAL SUN CONDITIONS: Full to partial sun

PHYSICAL APPEARANCE: Half the mature height of standard star magnolias, 'Kikuzaki' fits in just about any landscape. Multiple stems and low branching give this tree a shrubby appearance. In very early spring, a plethora of 2- to 3-inch–wide, pale pink to white flowers pop out of the bare branches. The blooms have a soft fragrance and are followed by glossy, dark green leaves that are lighter colored beneath. Its upright growth habit makes it ideal for planting next to patios, porches, and driveways.

CARE REQUIREMENTS: 'Kikuzaki' dwarf star magnolia requires well-drained soil and needs to be regularly watered until established. It blooms on old wood, so the buds are formed at the end of the previous season. If you must prune, do so just after blooming.

EXTRA INFO: Even young plants are prolific bloomers, but like other star magnolias, occasionally the buds or flowers may get damaged by hard spring frosts or winter winds. Planting in a sheltered site will help.

Evening Light Japanese Snowbell

COMMON NAME: Evening Light Japanese Snowbell

BOTANICAL NAME: *Styrax japonicus* 'Evening Light'

PLANT TYPE: Flowering tree; deciduous

MATURE DIMENSIONS: 10 feet tall; 5 feet wide

HARDINESS: Winter hardy down to −20°F (USDA Zones 5–9)

IDEAL SUN CONDITIONS: Full to partial sun

PHYSICAL APPEARANCE: The striking, dark purple leaves of this Japanese snowbell are awash in white, dangling, heavily fragrant, bell-shaped flowers in late spring and early summer, making it one of the most spectacular flowering displays on any small tree. And, if not subjected to drought, 'Evening Light' often reblooms in early fall! The beautiful, vase-like structure of this compact tree is oh so graceful.

CARE REQUIREMENTS: Japanese snowbells thrive in slightly acidic soils rich in organic matter. For maximum bloom power and the best leaf color, plant this petite tree in a sheltered site and keep it well watered, especially during the dry summer months. Prune just after flowering, if you must prune at all.

EXTRA INFO: Its repeat blooming habit makes this small tree extra special. I have one in my front yard, and the pollinators enjoy the dangling flowers as much as I do. Plus, the bark is beautiful in the winter.

Wedding Bells Carolina Silverbell

COMMON NAME: Wedding Bells Carolina Silverbell

BOTANICAL NAME: *Halesia carolina* 'UConn Wedding Bells'

PLANT TYPE: Flowering tree; deciduous

MATURE DIMENSIONS: 20 feet tall; 10 to 15 feet wide

HARDINESS: Winter hardy down to −20°F (USDA Zones 5–8)

IDEAL SUN CONDITIONS: Partial shade

PHYSICAL APPEARANCE: This tree is a slightly more compact form of our native North American Carolina silverbell, and its attractiveness cannot be overstated. The large, hanging blossoms are the reason 'Wedding Bells' is its cultivar name. An oval-shaped tree with fine branching, this Halesia's form is much like an elongated lollipop. Pure white, pendulous, bell-shaped flowers occur in mid-spring, followed by seeds with four "wings." This tree is best utilized as an understory specimen, as it prefers a protected, partially shaded environment.

CARE REQUIREMENTS: Select a planting site with rich, fertile, well-drained soil. Like other silverbells, slightly acidic soil is best.

EXTRA INFO: 'Wedding Bells' makes a striking specimen tree, but it does not tolerate salt, so don't place it near a road or sidewalk.

Slender Silhouette Sweetgum

COMMON NAME: Slender Silhouette Sweetgum

BOTANICAL NAME: *Liquidambar styraciflua* 'Slender Silhouette'

PLANT TYPE: Foliage tree; deciduous

MATURE DIMENSIONS: 30 to 40 feet tall; 4 to 6 feet wide

HARDINESS: Winter hardy down to −20°F (USDA Zones 5–8)

IDEAL SUN CONDITIONS: Full sun

PHYSICAL APPEARANCE: Few trees offer fall color as phenomenal as the sweetgum, but standard varieties are way too big for urban landscapes. This tall, thin cultivar changes all that. Its quick-growing, columnar habit is pretty spectacular. With classic sweetgum star-shaped leaves, 'Slender Silhouette' does produce the same round, prickly seed balls as other sweetgums, but not very prolifically. The unique growth habit of this tree will just about knock your socks off.

CARE REQUIREMENTS: Sweetgums are tolerant of a broad range of soil conditions. 'Slender Silhouette' requires little, if any, pruning and is very easy to grow. Water regularly until established.

EXTRA INFO: This is a cultivar of a North American native plant species that's indigenous to coastal regions of the eastern half of North America down to Central America. It will serve as a larval host plant for several species of butterflies and moths.

Amanogawa Japanese Flowering Cherry

COMMON NAME: Amanogawa Japanese Flowering Cherry

BOTANICAL NAME: *Prunus serrulata* 'Amanogawa'

PLANT TYPE: Flowering tree; deciduous

MATURE DIMENSIONS: 25 feet tall; 10 to 12 feet wide

HARDINESS: Winter hardy down to −20°F (USDA Zones 5–8)

IDEAL SUN CONDITIONS: Full to partial sun

PHYSICAL APPEARANCE: Another narrow, columnar tree for tight spaces, 'Amanogawa' Japanese flowering cherry blooms in early spring. It produces large, semidouble, subtly fragrant, soft pink flowers, followed by bronze-tinted spring foliage that ages to green. The orange fall color is notable as well.

CARE REQUIREMENTS: This Japanese flowering cherry requires regular irrigation until established or during drought. It's usually produced via grafting, so don't bury the tree too deeply or suckers may develop.

EXTRA INFO: This Japanese cultivar dates back to the 1880s. Its mature height is pretty standard for a Japanese flowering cherry, but its narrow width makes it a unique member of this extensive family.

Coralburst® Crabapple

COMMON NAME: Coralburst® Crabapple

BOTANICAL NAME: *Malus* × 'Coralcole'

PLANT TYPE: Flowering tree; deciduous

MATURE DIMENSIONS: 8 to 10 feet tall; 12 feet wide

HARDINESS: Winter hardy down to −30°F
(USDA Zones 4–8)

IDEAL SUN CONDITIONS: Full sun

PHYSICAL APPEARANCE: Absolutely smothered in semidouble, pink flowers in early spring, this slow-growing, compact crabapple is like no other. The flowers are followed by medium green, disease-resistant leaves and tiny, brownish red fruits that the birds relish. Great for courtyards, patio plantings, and pocket-sized yards.

CARE REQUIREMENTS: Coralburst® crabapples are easy to maintain. They require little to no pruning and are tolerant of a broad range of soil conditions. Drought tolerant once established. Avoid waterlogged soils in low-lying areas.

EXTRA INFO: Extremely resistant to scab, cedar-apple rust, and fireblight, Coralburst® is one of the finest crabapples on the market. It also makes a great pollinator plant for many edible apple varieties.

Little Gem Dwarf Southern Magnolia

COMMON NAME: Little Gem Dwarf Southern Magnolia

BOTANICAL NAME: *Magnolia grandiflora* 'Little Gem'

PLANT TYPE: Flowering tree; evergreen

MATURE DIMENSIONS: 20 to 25 feet tall; 10 to 15 feet wide

HARDINESS: Winter hardy down to 0°F (USDA Zones 7–9)

IDEAL SUN CONDITIONS: Full sun

PHYSICAL APPEARANCE: Like its full-sized kin, this compact southern magnolia is lush and attractive. The leaves are just as dark green and glossy as traditional southern magnolias, but they're smaller in size. Large, white, perfumed flowers cover this columnar cultivar in late spring through summer and may occur again in the fall in cooler climates.

CARE REQUIREMENTS: 'Little Gem' thrives in acidic, well-drained soil. Add granular, acid-specific fertilizer to the root zone every spring after the plant is established. Prune in winter if you must, but it's typically not necessary.

EXTRA INFO: While 'Little Gem' certainly isn't as petite as some of the other trees featured here, it is significantly smaller than a standard southern magnolia.

PERENNIALS

While there are plenty of perennials that are naturally short statured (many of which are used as ground covers or at the front of borders and beds), these are compact cultivars of plant species that are typically taller in stature.

Little Giant Purple Coneflower

COMMON NAME: Little Giant Purple Coneflower

BOTANICAL NAME: *Echinacea purpurea* 'Little Giant'

PLANT TYPE: Flowering perennial

MATURE DIMENSIONS: 12 to 18 inches tall; 1 foot wide

HARDINESS: Winter hardy down to −40°F (USDA Zones 3–8)

IDEAL SUN CONDITIONS: Full sun

BLOOM TIME: June through August

PHYSICAL APPEARANCE: This tiny-but-mighty coneflower is just as awesome as standard coneflower varieties when it comes to its pollinator prowess and good looks. Five-inch-wide flowers are borne atop short, stocky stems. The bright purply-pink petals surround an orange central disk. Dark foliage is deer resistant. This is a cultivar of a North American native plant.

CARE REQUIREMENTS: Coneflowers are native to moist prairies and meadows, but they're extremely tolerant of a broad range of growing conditions, including clay-based and dry soils. Divide 'Little Giant' every 4 to 5 years or whenever there's a decline in bloom numbers or the center of the plant starts dying out. This cultivar does not produce viable seeds. Deadhead every week or two to generate subsequent blooms, if desired.

Snowcap Shasta Daisy

COMMON NAME: Snowcap Shasta Daisy

BOTANICAL NAME: *Leucanthemum × superbum* 'Snowcap'

PLANT TYPE: Flowering perennial

MATURE DIMENSIONS: 10 to 14 inches tall; 12 inches wide

HARDINESS: Winter hardy down to −30°F (USDA Zones 4–9)

IDEAL SUN CONDITIONS: Full sun

BLOOM TIME: June through August

PHYSICAL APPEARANCE: Shastas are cherished for their bright white, classic daisy-like blooms and tough-as-nails nature, and 'Snowcap' offers all of that but in a smaller package. This dwarf variety does not flop, so there's no staking required. The foliage is dark and glossy, offering a mounding growth habit that stays neat and tidy. Flower stems are all the same height, making the plant look like a cushion of flowers when it's in bloom. This is an excellent plant for mass plantings.

CARE REQUIREMENTS: 'Snowcap' is a drought-, heat-, and humidity-tolerant hybrid. To care for it, simply shear back the flowering stems after blooming, if desired, and divide in the spring every few years. Select a planting site with moist, well-drained soil, though the plant isn't overly particular about growing conditions.

Grape Knee-Hi Lobelia

COMMON NAME: Grape Knee-Hi Lobelia

BOTANICAL NAME: *Lobelia × speciosa* 'Grape Knee-Hi'

PLANT TYPE: Flowering perennial

MATURE DIMENSIONS: 18 to 22 inches tall; 12 to 14 inches wide

HARDINESS: Winter hardy down to −20°F (USDA Zones 5–8)

IDEAL SUN CONDITIONS: Full sun

BLOOM TIME: July through September

PHYSICAL APPEARANCE: This little powerhouse plant attracts hummingbirds, butterflies, and other pollinators. It bears upright spires of purple-blue flowers that stand above a rosette of deep green foliage. This is a hybrid that makes a terrific mass planting and does not require staking to remain upright all season long.

CARE REQUIREMENTS: One of the best compact perennials for low-lying, wet garden areas, 'Grape Knee-Hi' shrugs off soggy roots and is an ideal plant for rain gardens and stream-side habitats. But, don't let that stop you from growing it in average garden soil, because it thrives there, too. A winter mulch of cut evergreen boughs will help see this lobelia through winters where the weather gets extremely cold.

Low Down Willowleaf Sunflower

COMMON NAME: Low Down Willowleaf Sunflower

BOTANICAL NAME: *Helianthus salicifolius* 'Low Down'

PLANT TYPE: Flowering perennial

MATURE DIMENSIONS: 12 to 18 inches tall; 18 to 24 inches wide

HARDINESS: Winter hardy down to −10°F (USDA Zones 6–9)

IDEAL SUN CONDITIONS: Full sun

BLOOM TIME: September and October

PHYSICAL APPEARANCE: A groundbreaking cultivar of a North American native plant, this micro-helianthus deserves to be prized by anyone and everyone who gardens in a postage stamp–sized yard. It's sunny and bold and everything that a perennial sunflower should be! Each blossom consists of a halo of yellow petals surrounding a brown center that's filled with small native bees all summer long. Dense clusters of flowers cover the entire plant, and the leaves are slender and downward curved. 'Low Down' willowleaf sunflower looks lovely in a vase or growing in a garden bed or container.

CARE REQUIREMENTS: Like full-sized helianthus, 'Low Down' tolerates clay soil, is deer resistant, and forms a sizeable clump fairly quickly. But, unlike the straight species, this cultivar seldom needs to be divided, pinched, or staked. The seeds of 'Low Down' are reportedly sterile.

King Edward Yarrow

COMMON NAME: King Edward Yarrow

BOTANICAL NAME: *Achillea × lewisii* 'King Edward'

PLANT TYPE: Flowering perennial

MATURE DIMENSIONS: 6 to 8 inches tall; 12 inches wide

HARDINESS: Winter hardy down to −40°F (USDA Zones 3–8)

IDEAL SUN CONDITIONS: Full sun

BLOOM TIME: June through August

PHYSICAL APPEARANCE: The low, carpet-like growth of this hybrid yarrow means it looks great even when the plant isn't in flower. But, when bloom-time does arrive, the mustard-yellow flowers are borne in clusters at the tops of stems that stand 6 inches above the foliage. The leaves are wooly and serrated and almost fern-like. 'King Edward' yarrow brightens up rock gardens, small perennial beds, and even sidewalk edges.

CARE REQUIREMENTS: Like other yarrows, 'King Edward' shrugs off heat and humidity, and tolerates salty seaside climates. Average garden soil is best. Give this plant room to spread and shear off dead flower stems after blooming to keep the plant looking tidy and generate a small flush of secondary blooms.

Little Spire Russian Sage

COMMON NAME: Little Spire Russian Sage

BOTANICAL NAME: *Perovskia atriplicifolia* 'Little Spire'

PLANT TYPE: Woody flowering perennial

MATURE DIMENSIONS: 18 to 24 inches tall; equal spread

HARDINESS: Winter hardy down to −30°F (USDA Zones 4–9)

IDEAL SUN CONDITIONS: Full sun

BLOOM TIME: June through frost

PHYSICAL APPEARANCE: A cutie-pie cultivar of an Asian native plant that's typically too floppy and wide spreading for smaller gardens, 'Little Spire' Russian sage offers the same wonderful color and long-lasting blooms as its relatives but in a compact form. Wispy, upright spires of blue flowers grace the gray-green foliage of these airy plants. At the end of the growing season, leave the plants in place; their silvery stalks offer winter interest to the garden as well.

CARE REQUIREMENTS: Both deer and rabbit resistant due to its highly fragranced foliage, 'Little Spire' is definitely a home run in the care department. Tolerant of dry soil and clay soil, all you have to do to care for the plant is cut it back to the ground in late winter or early spring. No pinching, dividing, or deadheading required.

Li'l Bang™ Red Elf Tickseed

COMMON NAME: Li'l Bang™ Red Elf Tickseed

BOTANICAL NAME: *Coreopsis* × *verticillata* 'Red Elf'

PLANT TYPE: Flowering perennial

MATURE DIMENSIONS: 12 inches tall; equal width

HARDINESS: Winter hardy down to −20°F (USDA Zones 5–9)

IDEAL SUN CONDITIONS: Full to partial sun

BLOOM TIME: June through September

PHYSICAL APPEARANCE: Li'l Bang™ coreopsis is a hybrid series derived from one of our North American native plants. There are several different colors in this series, but I like 'Red Elf' the best. Rich, velvety-red petals surround the bright yellow centers of its daisy-like blooms. This is a prolific bloomer that's adored by pollinators, long blooming, and disease resistant. Naturally compact, this perennial is also great for pots.

CARE REQUIREMENTS: Choose a well-drained site for the best performance and shear plants back after blooming to encourage a subsequent flush of blooms and tidy up the plant. Like other coreopsis, 'Red Elf' benefits from being divided every few years. The seeds are reportedly sterile.

Volcano® series of Phlox

COMMON NAME: Volcano® series of Phlox

BOTANICAL NAME: *Phlox paniculata* Volcano® series

PLANT TYPE: Flowering perennial

MATURE DIMENSIONS: 12 to 20 inches tall; 12 to 18 inches wide

HARDINESS: Winter hardy down to −30°F (USDA Zones 4–9)

IDEAL SUN CONDITIONS: Full to partial sun

BLOOM TIME: June through September

PHYSICAL APPEARANCE: Another series of cultivars derived from a North American native plant, Volcano® phlox comes in a broad range of colors, from lilac and pink to red and white. Large, ball-like clusters of ½-inch-wide, trumpet-shaped blooms grace the tops of strong, sturdy stems all summer long. No staking required! The blooms are adored by bees, butterflies, and hummingbirds; and they have a long life in both the garden and the vase. The entire Volcano® series is resistant to powdery mildew, making it a great choice for blocks of color in a tiny cottage garden or a more formal perennial bed.

CARE REQUIREMENTS: Cut off spent blooms, plus one-quarter of the stem growth, and this compact perennial will bloom again and again. Choose a well-drained site—soggy soils are a no-no—and be sure to regularly irrigate during extreme heat. Unfortunately, this plant is not deer or rabbit resistant, but it sure is gorgeous!

Leading Lady Plum Bee Balm

COMMON NAME: Leading Lady Plum Bee Balm

BOTANICAL NAME: *Monarda* × 'Leading Lady Plum'

PLANT TYPE: Flowering annual

MATURE DIMENSIONS: 10 to 14 inches tall; 2 to 3 feet wide

HARDINESS: Winter hardy down to −30°F (USDA Zones 4–8)

IDEAL SUN CONDITIONS: Full to partial sun

BLOOM TIME: June through September

PHYSICAL APPEARANCE: Though I'm particularly fond of the plum-colored cultivar of this hybrid plant, it also comes in other colors, including 'Leading Lady Lilac' and 'Leading Lady Orchid'. Earlier blooming than other bee balms, its clump-forming, compact habit means you can put it front and center without worrying about it taking over the entire garden. The magenta-purple flowers of 'Leading Lady Plum' are prized by butterflies, hummingbirds, and bumblebees. Plus, the blooms are edible, the foliage is fragrant, and when dried, both make a great herbal tea.

CARE REQUIREMENTS: Average garden soil will do just fine. Cut off spent blooms to generate a second flush of flowers in late summer. Though it isn't necessary, an early-spring pinching will keep this compact plant even shorter and delay its blooming by a few days. As with other Monardas, divide the plants when their center starts to die out. This is a hybrid of a North American native plant.

Purple Rock Candy® Beardlip Penstemon

COMMON NAME: Purple Rock Candy® Beardlip Penstemon

BOTANICAL NAME: *Penstemon barbatus* 'Novapenpur'

PLANT TYPE: Flowering perennial

MATURE DIMENSIONS: 8 to 12 inches tall; 18 to 24 inches wide

HARDINESS: Winter hardy down to −20°F (USDA Zones 5–8)

IDEAL SUN CONDITIONS: Full to partial sun

BLOOM TIME: June through July

PHYSICAL APPEARANCE: The bold, dark purple flowers of Purple Rock Candy® penstemon have a white throat that calls in pollinators. The upright flowering stems are packed with blooms from top to bottom, and they sit atop green, compact foliage. There are other varieties in the Rock Candy® series, including blue, light pink, and ruby. A cultivar of a western North American native plant, the ground-hugging foliage of this penstemon is partially evergreen, adding an extra layer of interest to the winter garden.

CARE REQUIREMENTS: To maintain this plant, simply trim off the flower stems as they age and a new flush of blooms will appear. Average garden soil is best for this heat- and drought-tolerant variety. Do not plant it in wet, poorly drained soils, however, or root rot will be the likely result.

Thumbelina Leigh English Lavender

COMMON NAME: Thumbelina Leigh English Lavender

BOTANICAL NAME: *Lavandula angustifolia* 'Thumbelina Leigh'

PLANT TYPE: Woody flowering perennial; evergreen

MATURE DIMENSIONS: 12 to 18 inches tall; 12 inches wide

HARDINESS: Winter hardy down to −20°F (USDA Zones 5–9)

IDEAL SUN CONDITIONS: Full sun

BLOOM TIME: June through August

PHYSICAL APPEARANCE: Nothing says summer like perfumed wands of lavender flowers. A compact selection of this aromatic herb, 'Thumbelina Leigh' is smothered in classic, purple-blue flowers up to three times a year, if the plant is pruned back after each flush of flowers. Disease-free, drought-tolerant, gray-green foliage is great for low-water gardens; but it's also suited to perennial borders, herb gardens, dry slopes, rock gardens, and shrub beds, too. In fact, you can't beat this lavender for container growing, either!

CARE REQUIREMENTS: 'Thumbelina Leigh' thrives in loose, fast-draining, gravelly soils and will sometimes rot when planted in heavy clay or waterlogged soils. Choose a site accordingly or grow it in a pot filled with a gravelly, sandy potting soil mix. Shear off the spent flowers and half of the growth just after blooming ends to generate a new flush of flowers. Trim the plant back hard in every early spring, just before new growth emerges.

Buzz™ Butterfly Bush Series

COMMON NAME: Buzz™ Butterfly Bush Series

BOTANICAL NAME: *Buddleja* hybrids Buzz™ series

PLANT TYPE: Woody flowering perennial

MATURE DIMENSIONS: 2 to 3 feet tall; equal spread

HARDINESS: Winter hardy down to −20°F (USDA Zones 5–11)

IDEAL SUN CONDITIONS: Full sun

BLOOM TIME: May through frost

PHYSICAL APPEARANCE: One-third the height of standard butterfly bush varieties, this series produces large flower heads on compact plants. Buzz™ butterfly bushes are early flowering and perfect for pots. Their light fragrance and panicles of tiny, trumpet-like blooms are attractive to butterflies and other pollinators. This series comes in a range of colors from ivory and purple to magenta and lavender.

CARE REQUIREMENTS: For the best performance, prune the plants back hard in the early spring, before new growth emerges. Then, trim off spent flowers to generate more blooms throughout the growing season. There's no need to pinch or stake this variety. Plus, it's drought and heat tolerant, once established.

Moody Blues® Dark Blue Speedwell

COMMON NAME: Moody Blues® Dark Blue Speedwell

BOTANICAL NAME: *Veronica spicata* 'Novaverblu'

PLANT TYPE: Flowering perennial

MATURE DIMENSIONS: 12 to 14 inches tall; equal spread

HARDINESS: Winter hardy down to −30°F (USDA Zones 4–9)

IDEAL SUN CONDITIONS: Full sun

BLOOM TIME: June through frost

PHYSICAL APPEARANCE: I can't say enough about this compact veronica. It's covered with dark purple-blue flower spikes all summer long; the color is outstanding. The densely packed flowers open from the bottom to the top of upright flower spikes that are very long lasting. There's also a pink and a white veronica in the Moody Blues® series. The foliage is deer resistant and blemish free, and the plant stays very neat and tidy all summer long.

CARE REQUIREMENTS: One established, Moody Blues® speedwell is very drought tolerant, thriving in well-drained, average garden soil. A weekly deadheading promotes new growth and flowering. Plants should be divided every 4 to 5 years.

Tiny Tortuga Turtlehead

COMMON NAME: Tiny Tortuga Turtlehead

BOTANICAL NAME: *Chelone obliqua* 'Tiny Tortuga'

PLANT TYPE: Flowering perennial

MATURE DIMENSIONS: 18 to 24 inches tall; 12 to 18 inches wide

HARDINESS: Winter hardy down to −30°F (USDA Zones 4–9)

IDEAL SUN CONDITIONS: Full to partial sun

BLOOM TIME: July through frost

PHYSICAL APPEARANCE: With large, hooded, pink flowers borne in clusters at the tops of the stems, this mini turtlehead is a garden wonder. The foliage is a glossy dark green to bronze, and it stands in an upright, rigid clump. There's no need to stake this plant, even in the shade. This cultivar of a North American native plant is lovely even when it isn't in flower.

CARE REQUIREMENTS: A low-maintenance workhorse, 'Tiny Tortuga' turtlehead is easy as can be. There's no need to pinch, prune, or deadhead. Like other turtleheads, this variety does excellent in moist, low-lying areas, making it ideal for woodland or bog gardens. It's slow to emerge from the ground in the spring, so give it some extra time. Turtlehead prefers soils high organic matter; work plenty of compost into the planting site.

Little Goldstar Black-Eyed Susans

COMMON NAME: Little Goldstar Black-Eyed Susans

BOTANICAL NAME: *Rudbeckia fulgida* var. *sullivantii* 'Little Goldstar'

PLANT TYPE: Flowering perennial

MATURE DIMENSIONS: 12 to 18 inches tall; equal spread

HARDINESS: Winter hardy down to −30°F (USDA Zones 4–9)

IDEAL SUN CONDITIONS: Full to partial sun

BLOOM TIME: July through September

PHYSICAL APPEARANCE: This knee-high version of a perennial favorite is oh so bright and cheerful! Who doesn't love black-eyed Susans? The flower stalks of 'Little Goldstar' are sturdy and upright. Each stalk is highly branched and produces several flowers, smothering the plant in yellow, daisy-like blooms with dark centers for weeks. A cultivar of a North American native plant, this variety hosts many pollinators when in bloom. The leaves are narrow, and the plant forms a cushion-like clump.

CARE REQUIREMENTS: Tolerant of a wide variety of soil conditions, 'Little Goldstar' also shrugs off hot, humid summers and drought with ease, though the plants should be kept well watered until established. No pinching or staking is necessary. Divide the plants every few years for improved performance.

Mariachi™ Helen's Flower

COMMON NAME: Mariachi™ Helen's Flower

BOTANICAL NAME: *Helenium autumnale* Mariachi™ series

PLANT TYPE: Flowering perennial

MATURE DIMENSIONS: 18 to 20 inches tall; 20 to 24 inches wide

HARDINESS: Winter hardy down to −40°F (USDA Zones 3–9)

IDEAL SUN CONDITIONS: Full sun

BLOOM TIME: June through September

PHYSICAL APPEARANCE: Helenium is definitely an underrated and underappreciated plant. But, in my mind, nothing compares to the festive blooms of this happy little plant. The Mariachi™ series of helenium offers colorful petals surrounding button-like centers. The varieties in this series bloom in several different shades, including bright red, orange-gold, and yellow. It's like a party in a plant! Heleniums boast outstanding late-season color and partner well with ornamental grasses and other fall bloomers, like asters and goldenrods. This group of cultivars is derived from a North American native plant and frequently visited by a diversity of pollinators.

CARE REQUIREMENTS: Mariachi™ heleniums prefer moist but well-drained garden soil. A wonderful addition to small-scale borders, beds, containers, and mass plantings, there's little necessary to maintain these plants. An early pinching encourages more branching and a higher number of flowers, but it isn't necessary. As an added bonus, the plants are deer resistant and the blooms are colorful additions to bouquets.

6

COMPACT PLANTS FOR THE FRUIT AND VEGETABLE GARDEN:

50 Profiles

There are so many wonderful compact edible plants, with more varieties being released onto the market every year. There's an increasing number of gardeners whose growing space is limited to a small area, such as a patio garden, a raised bed, or containers. Because of this, plant breeders and seed companies have dedicated much effort toward increasing the number of pint-sized fruits, veggies, and herbs available to home gardeners while also paying careful attention to flavor, disease resistance, and productivity, too.

The following edible plant profiles are designed to help you determine which petite varieties are best for your small-scale garden. Though there are many more choices not included on this list, these particular selections have performed well in my own garden over the years. In other words, these varieties are not just cutie-pie plants that are fun to look at; they're also resistant to common plant pathogens, easy to grow, high yielding, and delicious!

All of the plants on the following list require a minimum of 6 to 8 hours of full sun per day, with the exception of a few of the greens. If you're new to vegetable and fruit gardening, select a planting site that receives plenty of sun. You'll also want to avoid a location near large, established trees with extensive root systems that may outcompete your veggies (obviously this isn't a factor if you're growing in containers). Having the garden near a water source is helpful, too. Lugging the hose a great distance to water every few days is a big chore.

And now it's time to meet 50 of my favorite compact edible plants.

Baby Cakes® Blackberries

COMMON NAME: Baby Cakes® Blackberries

BOTANICAL NAME: *Rubus* × 'APF-236T'

MATURE DIMENSIONS: 3 to 4 feet tall; equally as wide

PHYSICAL APPEARANCE: Small-space gardeners have been out of luck when it comes to growing blackberries until this variety came along. Blackberries are notorious for their rambling, thorny vines, but Baby Cakes® is a thornless, dwarf blackberry that produces full-sized berries on compact plants. The dark, sweet berries are produced on old wood following clusters of white flowers.

PLANTING TIPS: Like other blackberries, this compact variety will spread, but not aggressively. Bred at the University of Arkansas, they're perfect for containers and raised beds. The flowers are self-fertile, so one plant is all you need for fruit set. Starter plants are available at garden centers. Space them 3 to 4 feet apart or one plant per 5-gallon container.

CARE REQUIREMENTS: Baby Cakes® blackberries are winter hardy down to −30°F. In late spring, prune out any canes that aren't showing new growth. Then, after harvest, prune canes that fruited to the ground and leave the newly developed canes, as they'll produce the next season's crop. This variety requires no staking or trellising. Overwinter potted specimens in a garage or shed, or by sinking the entire pot in the ground up to its rim.

HARVEST TIME: Mid- to late summer

Raspberry Shortcake® Raspberry

COMMON NAME: Raspberry Shortcake® Raspberry

BOTANICAL NAME: *Rubus idaeus* 'NR7'

MATURE DIMENSIONS: 2 to 3 feet tall; 3-foot spread

PHYSICAL APPEARANCE: These dwarf, thornless red raspberry plants aren't just cute; they're workhorses, too. The canes bear full-sized fruit in spite of their small stature. A rounded growth habit and lush, green foliage mean the plants are both pretty and productive.

PLANTING TIPS: Winter hardy down to −30°F, Raspberry Shortcake® berries are self-fertile, which means you'll get berries even if you only have one plant. Starter plants can be purchased from nurseries. Space them 3 to 4 feet apart or plant one plant per 5 gallon container.

CARE REQUIREMENTS: In late spring, prune out any stems that do not show signs of new growth. Leave any new growth intact because the canes produce fruit on the previous year's growth. New canes sprouting from ground may even produce fruit late in the same season. There's no staking or trellising required. Overwinter container-grown plants by putting them in a garage or shed, or by sinking the pot into the ground up to its rim.

HARVEST TIME: Summer and possibly a second crop in the fall

Jelly Bean® Blueberry

COMMON NAME: Jelly Bean® Blueberry

BOTANICAL NAME: *Vaccinium corymbosum* 'ZF06-179'

MATURE DIMENSIONS: 12 to 18 inches tall; equal spread

PHYSICAL APPEARANCE: Winter hardy down to −30°F, this plant produces large blueberries on a compact shrub. The leaves are elongated and have a touch of red. They also have a very pretty fall color. In spring, white to pink bell-shaped flowers appear, followed by plump berries in early summer.

PLANTING TIPS: Jelly Bean® blueberries make a great edible foundation plant or hedge. They're also great in containers. This variety can be purchased at garden centers. Space plants 4 to 5 feet apart or plant one shrub per 10-gallon container. Bumblebees and other pollinators love nectaring on the flowers. The plants are self-fertile, so only one plant is necessary for fruit set.

CARE REQUIREMENTS: Like other blueberries, Jelly Bean® prefers well-drained, acid soil. Use an acid-specific granular fertilizer every 2 years. Prune the plants annually to remove oldest stems and encourage new, productive wood. This variety requires a minimum of 1,000 chill hours (a chill hour is an hour at a temperature below 45°F), so northern climates suit it best. Blueberries have a very fibrous root system; mulch lightly with pine needles or 1 to 2 inches of bark mulch each spring. If grown in a pot, overwinter this blueberry in a garage or shed or sink the pot into the ground up to its rim.

HARVEST TIME: Early to midsummer

Blueberry Glaze® Blueberry

COMMON NAME: Blueberry Glaze® Blueberry

BOTANICAL NAME: *Vaccinium* × 'ZF08-095'

MATURE DIMENSIONS: 2 to 3 feet tall; equal spread

PHYSICAL APPEARANCE: The foliage and growth habit of Blueberry Glaze® make it look a lot like a boxwood, except it produces little, white, bell-shaped blooms, and dark, delicious fruit. This is an interspecies hybrid that requires fewer chill hours (a chill hour is an hour at a temperature below 45°F) than some other blueberries, making it suitable to all but the southernmost garden. The glossy leaves have a lovely fall color.

PLANTING TIPS: Winter hardy down to −20°F, this is a blueberry that makes a great hedge or foundation plant, in addition to containers or mass plantings. Plants are available in the nursery trade and should be planted 4 to 5 feet apart or one plant per 10-gallon container.

CARE REQUIREMENTS: Blueberry Glaze® is self-pollinating, so there's no need to have multiple varieties for fruit set. Fertilize with an acid-specific fertilizer every 2 years and prune in late winter to remove older canes. Potted plants must be overwintered in a garage or shed or sunk into the ground up to the pot's rim.

HARVEST TIME: Midsummer

Loran Strawberry

COMMON NAME: Loran Strawberry

BOTANICAL NAME: *Fragaria ananassa* 'Loran'

MATURE DIMENSIONS: 6 to 8 inches tall; 10 to 12 inches wide

PHYSICAL APPEARANCE: A perfectly petite strawberry that's at home in any landscape, 'Loran' is a European variety. Its early white flowers are followed by big fruit that's produced in waves off and on, all season long. The compact plants have lush green leaves, and the berries are cone-shaped and oh so sweet.

PLANTING TIPS: This ever-bearing variety provides a handful of berries every day, all season long. Plant them 6 inches apart to make an edible border, or tuck six of them in an 18-inch pot. They're winter hardy down to −20°F.

CARE REQUIREMENTS: 'Loran' produces few to no runners, so it's clump forming and not prone to spreading all over the garden. To overwinter the plants in the garden, use a straw mulch layer. For potted berries, move the container to a garage or shed or sink the pot into ground for the winter. Dig up and replace the plants every 4 to 5 years to rejuvenate your berry patch.

HARVEST TIME: Early summer through fall

Alpine Strawberry

COMMON NAME: Alpine Strawberry

BOTANICAL NAME: *Fragaria vesca*

MATURE DIMENSIONS: 6 to 8 inches tall; equal spread

PHYSICAL APPEARANCE: There are several different cultivars on the market, but all alpine strawberries bear small, super sweet berries that have a lovely fragrance. There are both red-fruited and white-fruited varieties, both of which offer an intense flavor. The ever-bearing nature of these plants means berries are produced off and on, all season long.

PLANTING TIPS: Alpine strawberry plants are easy to grow from seed and often produce the same year the seeds are sown. You can also grow them from transplants. Space the plants 10 to 12 inches apart, or plant six plants per 18-inch container. This fruit looks great as a groundcover, slope cover, bed edging, or in window boxes.

CARE REQUIREMENTS: Winter hardy down to −20°F, Alpine strawberries are tough little plants. Provide a winter mulch of straw and divide the plants every 3 to 4 years. These strawberries do not send out runners. If you grow them in containers, overwinter the pot in a garage or shed or sink the pot into the ground until spring's arrival.

HARVEST TIME: Summer through fall

Urban Apple® Columnar Apple

COMMON NAME: Urban Apple® Columnar Apple

BOTANICAL NAME: *Malus* × *domestica* Urban Apple®

MATURE DIMENSIONS: 8 to 10 feet tall; 2 feet wide

PHYSICAL APPEARANCE: A columnar, narrow apple tree that fits in the tightest of spaces? Yes, please! The Urban Apple® line of apple trees has full-sized leaves and fruits but is at home in even the tiniest of backyards. There are several different varieties, including Tasty Red™, Golden Treat™, Blushing Delight™, and Tangy Green™. The fruiting spurs are tight against the trunk and the branching is upright, making these trees exceptional choices for those looking to utilize vertical space. As an added bonus, the trees often bear fruit the first year of planting.

PLANTING TIPS: Not all apple varieties are suited to all climates. Apples require a set number of chill hours to produce flowers (a chill hour is an hour at a temperature below 45°F). Apple varieties that require a high number of chill hours can't be grown in warmer climates or they won't set buds, while those requiring a low number of chill hours are best for more southern regions where they won't flower too early and get frosted. Urban Apple® trees require between 800 and 1,200 chill hours for the best bud set, making them suitable for most gardens in USDA hardiness zones 4 through 8, a far broader range than many other apples. Space trees 4 to 5 feet apart, or plant one tree per 15- to 20-gallon container.

CARE REQUIREMENTS: Apples are not self-fertile; you'll need to have at least two different varieties in order for cross-pollination and fruit set to occur. Be sure to water Urban Apples® regularly until they're established. Prune the trees in the late winter.

HARVEST TIME: Summer through fall, depending on which variety is planted

Pix Zee™ Peach

COMMON NAME: Pix Zee™ Peach

BOTANICAL NAME: *Prunus persica* 'Pix Zee'

MATURE DIMENSIONS: 5 to 6 feet tall; 4 to 5 feet wide

PHYSICAL APPEARANCE: Pix Zee™ peach is a true genetic dwarf variety that produces full-sized foliage and fruit. It's simply spectacular! The peaches are freestone with yellow flesh and red-orange skin. The tree is covered with pink blossoms in the spring, and the peaches are firm and flavorful.

PLANTING TIPS: This peach variety requires fewer than 400 hours below 45°F (called chill hours) between November and March to develop flower buds. This means that the flowers may open too early in northern climates and be destroyed by spring frosts, but it also means that you can grow Pix Zee™ peaches in southern climates, where other peaches that require more chill hours may not thrive. Winter hardy down to −10°F, this peach is great for small kitchen gardens. It's grafted onto a different root stock, so don't bury too deeply or suckering may occur.

CARE REQUIREMENTS: Pix Zee™ is self-fertile, which means no cross-pollination is necessary; you'll get plenty of peaches with just one tree. Prune the trees in late winter and protect from frosts when in bloom. Potted trees can be overwintered in an unheated garage in the north, or sink the pot into the garden to overwinter outdoors.

HARVEST TIME: Midsummer

Necta Zee™ Nectarine

COMMON NAME: Necta Zee™ Nectarine

BOTANICAL NAME: *Prunus persica* var. *nucipersica* (or var. *nectarina*) 'Necta Zee'

MATURE DIMENSIONS: 4 to 5 feet tall; 3 to 4 feet wide

PHYSICAL APPEARANCE: This yellow-fleshed, freestone dwarf nectarine has smooth, red skin. Despite its small stature, Necta Zee™ is very productive, producing dozens of nectarines in a garden or container.

PLANTING TIPS: Requiring 400 or fewer chill hours below 45°F between November and March in order to develop flower buds, this variety may bloom too early in the north, but it's perfectly suited to warmer climes where other nectarines may prove more difficult to grow. The trees are winter hardy down to −10°F, and since no cross-pollination is necessary, only one tree is needed for good fruit production. Necta Zee™ is grafted onto a different root stock; don't bury too deeply or suckering may occur.

CARE REQUIREMENTS: If frost threatens when the tree is in bloom, cover with a frost cloth or bedsheet to protect it. In cold climates, overwinter potted trees in a garage or sink the pot in the ground up to its rim. Prune in late winter.

HARVEST TIME: Midsummer

Pixie™ Grapes

COMMON NAME: Pixie™ Grapes

BOTANICAL NAME: *Vitis vinifera*

MATURE DIMENSIONS: 18 to 24 inches tall; 12 inches wide

PHYSICAL APPEARANCE: If you've always wanted to grow grapes but don't think you have the room, this line of dwarf grape plants is the answer! Originally developed for research purposes, their short internodes mean they produce lots of flowers instead of long, vining tendrils. There are several different varieties available, including Pinot Meunier, Riesling, and Cabernet Franc. These perfectly petite grape vines are ideal for urban gardens. The fruit clusters are about 4 to 5 inches long and quite tasty.

PLANTING TIPS: Winter hardy down to −30°F, Pixie™ grapes can be grown in the ground with a plant spacing of 3 to 4 feet or in a pot with one plant per 3-gallon container.

CARE REQUIREMENTS: Though the plants stay compact, you'll need to provide them with a vertical support or the grape clusters will sit on the ground. A small trellis will do. Fertilize the vines with a complete, granular, organic fertilizer every 5 weeks; but stop in midsummer to slow growth and ripen the fruit. To overwinter potted plants, move the pot into a cold garage or bury it in the soil up to its rim. Prune the vines in late winter.

HARVEST TIME: Summer through early fall

Peas-in-a-Pot Sweet Peas

COMMON NAME: Peas-in-a-Pot Sweet Peas

BOTANICAL NAME: *Pisum sativum* var. *sativum* 'Peas-in-a-pot'

MATURE DIMENSIONS: 10 inches tall; 4 inches wide

PHYSICAL APPEARANCE: These peas are cute as can be! Tiny plants bear 3- to 4-inch-long pods filled with plump green peas. The white flowers look lovely in mixed-container plantings, and as long as you regularly harvest the pods, production will continue until hot weather arrives.

PLANTING TIPS: Peas are a cool-season crop. Sow seeds directly into the garden in early spring for an early summer harvest or late summer for a fall harvest. Plant peas 1 inch deep and 2 inches apart. Use pea inoculant to improve the germination and growth of all pea varieties (this is especially important if you grow peas in pots).

CARE REQUIREMENTS: 'Peas-in-a-pot' sweet peas mature in 60 to 65 days from the sow date. There's no need to stake these little marvels. Harvest when the pods are swollen but still green.

HARVEST TIME: Early summer or late fall

Little SnapPea Crunch Sugar Snap Peas

COMMON NAME: Little SnapPea Crunch Sugar Snap Peas

BOTANICAL NAME: *Pisum sativum* var. *macrocarpon* 'Little SnapPea Crunch'

MATURE DIMENSIONS: 24 to 28 inches tall; 8 to 12 inches wide

PHYSICAL APPEARANCE: This edible-podded snap pea produces a plethora of plump, sweet pods on plants that are about a third the height of standard varieties. Three-inch-long pods follow lovely white flowers. The plants are fairly heat tolerant, too.

PLANTING TIPS: Peas are a cool-season crop, so sowing very early or late in the season is essential. Sow seeds directly into the garden or container, 1 inch deep and 2 inches apart. Use pea inoculant to improve the growth and germination of all pea varieties, especially if you're growing in containers. 'Little SnapPea Crunch' looks great mixed into flower borders, in containers, or in raised beds.

CARE REQUIREMENTS: There's no need to stake this variety, as the compact vines are self-supporting. Pods are ready to harvest when they're swollen and the peas inside have filled out, about 58 to 60 days after planting.

HARVEST TIME: Early summer or late fall

On Deck Sweet Corn

COMMON NAME: On Deck Sweet Corn

BOTANICAL NAME: *Zea mays* convar. *saccharata* var. *rugosa* 'On Deck'

MATURE DIMENSIONS: 4 to 5 feet tall; 12 to 18 inches wide

PHYSICAL APPEARANCE: If you don't think you have enough room to grow sweet corn, you'd be wise to think again. 'On Deck' is a super sweet, hybrid, bicolor corn bred just for small gardens and containers. Each plant produces two to three ears that are 7 to 8 inches long. It has a classic corn plant look, but at half the height of standard varieties.

PLANTING TIPS: Corn is wind pollinated, so you'll have to plant this crop in groups of at least 10 plants for decent kernel formation. The soil must be over 60°F before planting seeds or they may fail to germinate. Plant the seeds only after the danger of frost has passed. Seeds are sown 1 inch deep and 5 inches apart. If you choose to grow 'On Deck' in a container, be sure to select a large pot that can hold at least 10 to 12 full-grown stalks.

CARE REQUIREMENTS: Plants do not need to be staked, but don't plant 'On Deck' near other varieties of corn or cross-pollination could occur and cause the kernels to be starchy. Separate corn varieties by at least 250 feet; that includes any nearby field corn. The ears are ready for harvest 60 to 65 days after seeding.

HARVEST TIME: Mid- to late summer

Blue Jade Dwarf Corn

COMMON NAME: Blue Jade Dwarf Corn

BOTANICAL NAME: *Zea mays* convar. *saccharata* var. *rugosa* 'Blue Jade'

MATURE DIMENSIONS: 3 feet tall; 10 inches wide

PHYSICAL APPEARANCE: The stalks of this variety are half the height of traditional sweet corn varieties, and the kernels are an amazing deep steel blue at maturity! 'Blue Jade' is an open-pollinated heirloom sweet corn that's been grown for generations. The ears are ready to harvest 70 to 80 days after sowing, with each cob measuring 4 to 5 inches long.

PLANTING TIPS: Sow seeds directly into garden soil only after it's reached 60°F and the danger of frost has passed. Plant seeds 1 inch deep and 6 inches apart. Corn is wind pollinated, so you'll need to plant 'Blue Jade' in a block of at least 20 plants for good kernel set.

CARE REQUIREMENTS: The stalks are self-supporting, but they're also heavy feeders. Add supplemental fertilizer in the spring. To avoid accidental cross-pollination that will likely result in starchy kernels, isolate 'Blue Jade' from other corn varieties by at least 250 feet.

HARVEST TIME: Mid- to late summer

Baby Ball Beets

COMMON NAME: Baby Ball Beets

BOTANICAL NAME: *Beta vulgaris* 'Baby Ball'

MATURE DIMENSIONS: 8 inches tall; 5 inches wide

PHYSICAL APPEARANCE: 'Baby Ball' is a Dutch variety of petite beets that's an amazing gourmet treat. The perfect red orbs are sweet and tender, and they measure just 1 to 1½ inches in diameter. Ready to harvest 45 to 55 days after sowing, 'Baby Ball's' greens are edible, too.

PLANTING TIPS: Beets can be planted anytime the ground can be worked in early spring through late summer. Sow seeds directly into the garden or a container ½ inch deep and 2 to 3 inches apart. Each beet seed contains multiple embryos, so when the seedlings are about 1 inch tall, thin them to give each root plenty of room to grow.

CARE REQUIREMENTS: For optimum germination, keep the soil evenly moist. Beets are fairly cold tolerant. Protect the plants from frosts with floating row cover or a cold frame to prolong the harvest well into fall and early winter.

HARVEST TIME: Late spring though early winter

Tiara Cabbage

COMMON NAME: Tiara Cabbage

BOTANICAL NAME: *Brassica oleracea* var. *capitata* 'Tiara'

MATURE DIMENSIONS: 10 to 12 inches tall; 12 to 18 inches wide

PHYSICAL APPEARANCE: 'Tiara' is a beautiful hybrid minicabbage variety. It's early to produce, and its small, tight, round heads average 3 pounds each. Each cabbage produces a beautiful rosette of leaves that surrounds the head. 'Tiara' is perfect for high-density plantings or in small areas or containers.

PLANTING TIPS: It's best to start seeds indoors under grow lights 10 to 12 weeks before your last expected spring frost. Cabbage is a cool-season crop that's quite tolerant of light frosts. The transplants can go out into the garden when they're about 6 weeks old. Space plants 12 to 18 inches apart or plant one plant per 3-gallon pot. 'Tiara' also can be grown as a fall crop.

CARE REQUIREMENTS: Be sure to keep the soil evenly moist. If you provide a lot of water after a dry spell, the heads may crack open. Mulching helps prevent this. 'Tiara' requires 50 days to mature from transplant. To harvest cabbage, cut the head from plant using a sharp knife.

HARVEST TIME: Midsummer through fall in the north, fall through spring in the south

Thumbelina Carrot

COMMON NAME: Thumbelina Carrot

BOTANICAL NAME: *Daucus carota* subsp. *sativus* 'Thumbelina'

MATURE DIMENSIONS: 8 to 10 inches tall; 3 inches wide

PHYSICAL APPEARANCE: If ever there were a prize for the most adorable carrot, 'Thumbelina' would get the blue ribbon. These small, round carrots are bright orange and sweet enough to be eaten raw or cooked. An open-pollinated variety, 'Thumbelina's' skin is so thin it doesn't need to be peeled. This golf ball–sized carrot is ideal for gardens with rocky or heavy clay-based soils. It also does great in patio pots.

PLANTING TIPS: To plant carrots, sow seeds directly into the ground anytime from early spring through early autumn. Carrots grow well in both cool and warm seasons, though young plants won't do well in excessive summer heat. Sow seeds ¼ inch deep and 1 inch apart, but thin the seedlings to a 3-inch spacing when they're young. Be warned that carrot seeds take a long time to germinate, sometimes over 2 weeks.

CARE REQUIREMENTS: 'Thumbelina' carrots are easy to grow and ready to harvest just 60 days after planting. Mulch the rows to conserve moisture, and mound soil up over the "shoulders" of near-mature carrots to keep them from turning green.

HARVEST TIME: Early summer through late fall

Little Finger Carrot

COMMON NAME: Little Finger Carrot

BOTANICAL NAME: *Daucus carota* subsp. *sativus* 'Little Finger'

MATURE DIMENSIONS: 6 inches tall; 3 inches wide

PHYSICAL APPEARANCE: 'Little Finger' is the perfect name for this baby-type carrot that grows only as wide as a finger. Plus, it's so crunchy! The slender, 4-inch-long, bright orange roots are well suited to canning and pickling. Its thin skin and sweet flavor make this carrot a gourmet delight.

PLANTING TIPS: Carrot seeds are best planted directly into the garden or a deep container anytime from very early spring through late summer. The roots are ready for harvest 55 days after planting. Sow seeds ¼ inch deep and 1 inch apart, then thin the seedlings to 2 to 3 inches apart. Carrot seeds are very slow to germinate; sometimes it takes 2 to 3 weeks.

CARE REQUIREMENTS: Get rid of any rocks or lumpy soil prior to planting or the roots will fork or be misshapen. Keep the seedbed evenly moist and mulch the roots to keep weed competition at a minimum. Sow more seeds every few weeks for a continual harvest.

HARVEST TIME: Early summer through late fall

French Mascotte Bush Bean

COMMON NAME: French Mascotte
Bush Bean

BOTANICAL NAME: *Phaseolus vulgaris*
'French Mascotte'

MATURE DIMENSIONS: 20 inches tall; 16 inches wide

PHYSICAL APPEARANCE: 'French Mascotte' is more
than just a pretty plant. It produces long, slender
green beans that are held atop lush green foliage.
Its white to lavender flowers are lovely, too. A
French variety that's both incredibly productive
and disease resistant, the straight beans are 5
inches long, stringless, and delectably flavored.

PLANTING TIPS: Seeds are best planted directly into
the garden or a container after the danger of
frost has passed and nighttime temperatures stay
above 55°F. Plant them 1 inch deep and 4 inches
apart. Soaking the seeds for a few hours prior
to planting speeds the germination rate but isn't
necessary. Beans are ready for harvest 54 days
after planting.

CARE REQUIREMENTS: Like many other green bean
varieties, the more you pick 'French Mascotte',
the more beans the plants will produce. The
pods are very easy to harvest due to the way
the beans grow above the plant tops. This bush
variety does not need to be staked or otherwise
supported.

HARVEST TIME: Summer

Patio Snacker Cucumber

COMMON NAME: Patio Snacker Cucumber

BOTANICAL NAME: *Cucumis sativus* 'Patio Snacker'

MATURE DIMENSIONS: 10 to 12 inches tall; 2 to 3 feet wide

PHYSICAL APPEARANCE: Once you grow this compact cuke, you'll be hooked. It's hard to believe how many 6-inch-long, slender fruits are produced on such small plants. With very short vines, this hybrid variety is ideal for pots and itty-bitty backyards. Like other cucumbers, the plants bear separate male and female flowers. But unlike many other varieties, 'Patio Snacker' doesn't need to have a lot of pollinators around to produce fruit. The flowers are parthenocarpic, meaning they have the ability to set fruit without insect pollination, making this an excellent choice for urban areas and balcony gardens where pollinators may be in limited supply.

PLANTING TIPS: 'Patio Snacker' cucumbers are ready to harvest just 55 days after planting the seeds. Wait to plant until the soil temp reaches at least 65°F and the danger of frost has passed. Sow seeds ½ to 1 inch deep and space plants 3 feet apart, or plan on one plant per 3-gallon container.

CARE REQUIREMENTS: Use a small trellis or fence to support the vines, or let them spill out over the edge of a container. Harvest the cucumbers on a continual basis for more production. With all cucumbers, consistent, even moisture is critical for good fruit development.

HARVEST TIME: Summer through fall

Salad Bush Cucumber

COMMON NAME: Salad Bush Cucumber

BOTANICAL NAME: *Cucumis sativus* 'Salad Bush'

MATURE DIMENSIONS: 2 feet tall; equally as wide

PHYSICAL APPEARANCE: A bush type that doesn't vine, this hybrid cuke needs very little space to perform its best. A plethora of 8-inch-long, uniform cucumbers are produced on each disease-resistant plant.

PLANTING TIPS: Sow seeds directly into the garden or containers when the danger of frost has passed and the soil temperature has reached 60°F. Sow more seeds every few weeks to extend your harvest well into the autumn. Seeds are best planted ½ to 1 inch deep and 2 feet apart. Cucumbers resent transplanting, so if you choose to start seeds early indoors, be sure to use plantable peat pots so you won't disturb the roots when moving the plants into the garden.

CARE REQUIREMENTS: With its high disease resistance, 'Salad Bush' requires very little care. A 2-inch-thick layer of mulch keeps the soil consistently moist. At harvest time, cut the fruit from the vine; do not pull it. 'Salad Bush' is ready to harvest 57 days after planting.

HARVEST TIME: Summer through fall

Fairy Tale Eggplant

COMMON NAME: Fairy Tale Eggplant

BOTANICAL NAME: *Solanum melongena* 'Fairy Tale'

MATURE DIMENSIONS: 18 to 24 inches tall; 12 to 18 inches wide

PHYSICAL APPEARANCE: An adorable hybrid eggplant that produces small, 2- to 4-inch-long fruits, 'Fairy Tale' is a small-space gardener's dream. The lavender eggplants are streaked with white, have very few seeds, and are bitter free. The fruits are borne in clusters that hang from the plants. So pretty!

PLANTING TIPS: To grow this eggplant, sow seeds indoors under grow lights 6 to 8 weeks before the last expected frost date. Move the plants out into garden only after the danger of frost has passed. Space plants 18 inches apart or plant one plant per 3-gallon container.

CARE REQUIREMENTS: Plan to stake the plants or use cages to keep them upright and to keep the fruits off the ground. The eggplants are ready to cut from the plants 65 days after moving the transplants into the garden. At harvest time, the skin is glossy but the flesh gives a little under pressure from your thumb. If the skin is yellow tinted, the fruits are overripe.

HARVEST TIME: Summer through fall

Patio Baby Eggplant

COMMON NAME: Patio Baby Eggplant

BOTANICAL NAME: *Solanum melongena* 'Patio Baby'

MATURE DIMENSIONS: 16 to 24 inches tall; equal spread

PHYSICAL APPEARANCE: These compact hybrid plants are great for patio pots and urban gardens. Dark purple, egg-shaped, glossy fruits are 2 to 3 inches long and wide. Their thin skins make them great for roasting. Each plant produces many small fruits per cluster. This is a great variety for short growing seasons.

PLANTING TIPS: Sow seeds indoors under grow lights 6 to 8 weeks before the last expected frost date. Then, move plants outdoors when danger of frost has passed. Space the plants about 18 inches apart or plant one plant per 3-gallon container.

CARE REQUIREMENTS: The more you harvest, the more fruits this variety sets; and since the plants are spineless, picking is easy. Compact plants mean no staking is necessary. When ripe, cut the fruits from the plant; do not tear. 'Patio Baby' is ready to harvest just 50 days after transplanting out into the garden.

HARVEST TIME: Summer through early fall

Little Gem Lettuce

COMMON NAME: Little Gem Lettuce

BOTANICAL NAME: *Lactuca sativa* var. *longifolia* 'Little Gem'

MATURE DIMENSIONS: 8 to 10 inches tall; 6 inches wide

PHYSICAL APPEARANCE: 'Little Gem' is the cutest lettuce ever! It's a very small Romaine-type lettuce with green, crunchy leaves and a super sweet flavor. Surprisingly heat tolerant, each plant makes one perfect little salad. The upright habit and firm head make this little beauty a true garden treasure.

PLANTING TIPS: 'Little Gem' is easy to grow by sowing the seeds directly into the garden in early spring or late summer. Sow more seeds every 2 weeks for a continual harvest. Plant the seeds ¼ inch deep and 3 inches apart, then thin the seedlings to a spacing of 5 inches on center. Give summer sowings some shade to keep the plants from bolting and turning bitter.

CARE REQUIREMENTS: A variety that's ready to harvest just 50 days after sowing the seeds, 'Little Gem' needs to be well watered, especially during warm weather. To harvest, cut the entire head off at the ground or snap off just a few outer leaves at a time for a cut-and-come-again harvest.

HARVEST TIME: Late spring through fall in the north, fall through spring in the south

Dwarf Blue Curled Vates Kale

COMMON NAME: Dwarf Blue Curled Vates Kale

BOTANICAL NAME: *Brassica oleracea* 'Dwarf Blue Curled'

MATURE DIMENSIONS: 12 inches tall; equally as wide

PHYSICAL APPEARANCE: This low-growing kale fills the garden with ruffled, bluish-green leaves. It's cold tolerant and excellent when eaten cooked or raw. Kale is a cool-weather crop that's best for spring or fall plantings. This is a seriously beautiful, curly leaved plant that is as ornamental as it is delicious.

PLANTING TIPS: 'Dwarf Blue Curled' kale is easiest to plant via direct sowing. Sow seeds ¼ inch deep and 3 inches apart. Thin to an 8-inch spacing. This compact kale can be planted anytime in the spring as soon as the soil can be worked; about 2 to 4 weeks before the last expected frost is ideal. Late summer plantings result in fall and winter harvests. In warm southern regions, fall sowings are best.

CARE REQUIREMENTS: Ready to harvest just 55 days after planting from seed, 'Dwarf Blue Curled' is easy to protect from frosts with a layer of floating row cover, if you want to plant early or extend your fall harvest. Frost sweetens the flavor, so many gardeners relish late-season plantings. Harvest just the outer leaves and leave the growing point intact, or harvest the entire plant all at once.

HARVEST TIME: Late spring through early winter in the north; winter in the south

Pot of Gold Swiss Chard

COMMON NAME: Pot of Gold Swiss Chard

BOTANICAL NAME: *Beta vulgaris* subsp. *vulgaris* 'Pot of Gold'

MATURE DIMENSIONS: 12 to 15 inches tall; 8 to 10 inches wide

PHYSICAL APPEARANCE: Beautiful golden yellow stems and thick, succulent, green leaves make 'Pot of Gold' swiss chard a real superstar. Among the most reliable crops, chard is easy to grow, striking to look at, and flavorful in the kitchen. The lush, vase-shaped plants look great in gardens and containers.

PLANTING TIPS: Chard is best planted from seed sown directly into the garden or container anytime from early spring through late summer. Southern gardeners can grow it all winter long. If you're growing chard in a pot, choose a deep container. Sow seeds ½ inch deep and 1 inch apart, then thin the seedlings to 8 to 10 inches as they mature. Baby greens can be used in salads in as little as 30 days, while mature leaves take about 50 days from seed.

CARE REQUIREMENTS: Highly frost tolerant, chard is one of the easiest early-season crops to grow. But, keep the bunnies and deer away from the plants, as they seem to enjoy chard as much as people do! Harvest the outermost leaves on a regular basis, and leave the growing point intact for a continuous harvest. Cover the plants with a floating row cover for an extended harvest through the fall and early winter.

HARVEST TIME: Spring through summer in the north; fall through spring in the south

Extra Dwarf Pak Choy (Pak Choi/Bok Choy)

COMMON NAME: Extra Dwarf Pak Choy (Pak Choi/Bok Choy)

BOTANICAL NAME: *Brassica rapa* subsp. *chinensis* 'Extra Dwarf'

MATURE DIMENSIONS: 2 to 3 inches tall; equal spread

PHYSICAL APPEARANCE: 'Extra Dwarf' pak choy is about the most adorable veggie you can grow! Picked when it's just 2 to 3 inches tall, the deep green leaves, crisp midribs, and thick, white petioles (leaf stems) are excellent stir-fried or sautéed. The compact heads of this Asian green are fast to mature in just 30 days from seed.

PLANTING TIPS: To plant, sow seeds out in the garden ¼ inch deep and 1 inch apart. Thin to a spacing of 4 inches on center. This cool-season plant is best planted very early or very late in the season to avoid bolting. It does not tolerate heat and resents transplanting. Warm-climate gardeners can grow this pak choy all winter long.

CARE REQUIREMENTS: Keep seed bed evenly moist, and protect early and late plantings with a layer of floating row cover. Harvest the entire head by cutting it off at ground level.

HARVEST TIME: Mid- to late spring in the north; fall to early spring in the south

Little Hero Spinach

COMMON NAME: Little Hero Spinach

BOTANICAL NAME: *Spinacia oleracea* 'Little Hero'

MATURE DIMENSIONS: 2 inches tall; 5 inches wide

PHYSICAL APPEARANCE: The short, dark green, crunchy leaves of 'Little Hero' spinach are best picked baby sized. Its nutty flavor and succulent texture make this compact spinach a real winner. Plus, it's fast growing, maturing in just 40 days from seed.

PLANTING TIPS: Spinach is a cool-season crop. Plant seeds in the very early spring for spring harvests; or plant in the fall for fall and a subsequent spring harvest. In all but the extreme north, the plants readily overwinter when seeds are sown in the fall. In the south, 'Little Hero' can be grown all winter long. To plant, sow seeds ½ inch deep and 2 inches apart. Then, thin to a 6-inch spacing. Another option is to sow the seeds thickly and grow a solid bed of baby greens for scissor harvest.

CARE REQUIREMENTS: It's important to keep the seedbed well watered prior to germination. Multiple harvests can be made from the same planting as long as the growing points are left intact. Eventually, the plants will bolt when the weather gets hot and the days grow long. When this happens, pull up the plants.

HARVEST TIME: Mid-spring or fall in the north; fall through spring in the south

Long Island Semidwarf Brussels Sprouts

COMMON NAME: Long Island Semidwarf Brussels Sprouts

BOTANICAL NAME: *Brassica oleracea* var. *gemmifera* 'Long Island'

MATURE DIMENSIONS: 20 to 24 inches tall; 12 inches wide

PHYSICAL APPEARANCE: An heirloom brussels sprout that produces tons of mini cabbage-like sprouts all along the stem, 'Long Island' is an old variety that was once a staple garden crop. It has leaves that are tightly spaced, and each node produces a single sprout. Since the plants are compact and very upright, the stems do not need to be supported. This semidwarf brussels sprout variety is one-third to one-half the height of full-sized varieties.

PLANTING TIPS: Start seeds indoors under grow lights in late winter, about 10 weeks prior to your last expected frost date. The cold-tolerant transplants can move out into the garden as soon as the soil can be worked in the early spring. Seeds can also be sown directly into the garden in spring but must be thinned to a spacing of 15 inches.

CARE REQUIREMENTS: 'Long Island' takes about 90 to 100 days to reach maturity, so it requires a long growing season. Spring plantings aren't harvested until the autumn. In the south, brussels sprouts are a winter crop. Harvest the sprouts after a frost, which sweetens their flavor. To pick, twist or cut the sprouts off the stem. Sprouts can be harvested just a handful at a time or all at once.

HARVEST TIME: Fall in the north; spring in the south

Baby Bubba Okra

COMMON NAME: Baby Bubba Okra

BOTANICAL NAME: *Abelmoschus esculentus* 'Baby Bubba'

MATURE DIMENSIONS: 3 to 4 feet tall; 1 foot wide

PHYSICAL APPEARANCE: Okra is typically a large plant with a deep tap root, but this hybrid dwarf variety is only half as tall as standard okra and its root system is far less aggressive. A prolific producer of 2- to 3-inch-long, green pods, 'Baby Bubba' has lush green leaves with red stems and white flowers that are centered with a splash of red.

PLANTING TIPS: Ready for harvest in just 53 days, seeds are best sown directly into the garden after the danger of frost has passed and the soil has warmed. Plant seeds 1 inch deep and 10 inches apart. Or, start seeds indoors under grow lights 6 weeks before your average frost-free date and move the transplants outdoors after frosts end. You can also grow one plant per 2-gallon container. This variety is early to bear compared to other okras, making it great for both the north and the south.

CARE REQUIREMENTS: Mulch the plants with straw or shredded leaves to keep the roots cool and moist, and limit weeds. Harvest the pods by cutting them from the stems every few days to encourage further production.

HARVEST TIME: Summer through fall

Mohawk Patio Peppers

COMMON NAME: Mohawk Patio Peppers

BOTANICAL NAME: *Capsicum annuum* 'Mohawk'

MATURE DIMENSIONS: 8 to 10 inches tall; 10 to 12 inches wide

PHYSICAL APPEARANCE: Compact plants with 4-inch-long, thick-walled fruits that start green and ripen to a rich orange, 'Mohawk' is a very productive compact variety. The peppers are shaped like an elongated bell, and the plants are highly branched.

PLANTING TIPS: It takes this hybrid selection 75 days to reach maturity. 'Mohawk' looks great in hanging baskets and containers as well as in the garden. Sow seeds indoors under grow lights 8 weeks before the last spring frost, then transplant outdoors after the danger of frost has passed. Space the plants 18 inches apart in the garden or plant one transplant per 3-gallon container.

CARE REQUIREMENTS: Choose a well-drained area high in organic matter for planting. Like other peppers, 'Mohawk' may drop blossoms when temperatures are very hot. Its slightly trailing habit means there's no need to stake; just let the plants tumble.

HARVEST TIME: Summer through fall

Pizza My Heart Peppers

COMMON NAME: Pizza My Heart Peppers

BOTANICAL NAME: *Capsicum annuum*
'Pizza My Heart'

MATURE DIMENSIONS: 2 to 3 feet tall;
12 to 18 inches wide

PHYSICAL APPEARANCE: These conical peppers ripen to a glossy, brilliant red and their flavor is supreme. Very prolific and early to produce, 'Pizza My Heart' peppers have a slight heat.

PLANTING TIPS: Sow seeds indoors under grow lights 8 weeks before the last expected frost. Seeds may take up to 4 weeks to germinate. When nighttime temps reach 55°F consistently, move the plants into the garden, spacing them 18 inches apart or planting one transplant per 3-gallon pot.

CARE REQUIREMENTS: Requires 80 days from transplant to harvest, and staking or caging may be necessary when branches are laden with fruits. Mulch the plants to keep the soil moist and avoid blossom end rot. Harvest the peppers when they're fully colored by cutting them from the plant.

HARVEST TIME: Summer through fall

Tom Thumb Popcorn

COMMON NAME: Tom Thumb Popcorn

BOTANICAL NAME: *Zea mays* var. *everta* 'Tom Thumb'

MATURE DIMENSIONS: 3 to 4 feet tall; 18 inches wide

PHYSICAL APPEARANCE: This crazy little popcorn is half the height of full-sized popcorn varieties but surprisingly productive, making it a great choice for backyard gardeners. It produces one or two 4-inch-long ears per stalk, and its quick maturity (85 days) makes it great for short-season areas. 'Tom Thumb' yields yellow kernels that are popped into flavorful popcorn.

PLANTING TIPS: To grow this dwarf popcorn, plant seeds 1 inch deep and 4 inches apart in rows spaced 2 feet apart. You'll need a block of plants for good pollination and ear production rather than a single long row. If you grow 'Tom Thumb' in containers, make sure you have several dozen plants to ensure there's ample pollen in the air. Wait to plant the seeds until soil has warmed to 65°F and frost no longer threatens.

CARE REQUIREMENTS: An old variety from the mid-1800s, these dwarf plants are great for even cold climates, but do not plant 'Tom Thumb' near other varieties of corn to avoid cross-pollination and poor quality (a 500-foot separation is best). Allow the cobs to fully dry on the stalks before harvest, then lay the husked ears on a piece of newspaper in a dry room for a month before storing the cobs or loose kernels in an airtight container prior to popping.

HARVEST TIME: Late summer

Orange Cutie Pumpkins

COMMON NAME: Orange Cutie Pumpkins

BOTANICAL NAME: *Cucurbita maxima* 'Orange Cutie'

MATURE DIMENSIONS: 12 to 18 inches tall; 6 to 7 feet wide

PHYSICAL APPEARANCE: Pumpkin vines are notorious for taking over the garden, but this semibush hybrid variety has vines that are only one-third as long as standard pumpkin vines. Each 'Orange Cutie' plant produces 8 to 10 fruits that are orange with paler orange streaks on the midribs. Measuring 6 inches across and 5 inches tall, the pumpkins are great for both decoration and eating.

PLANTING TIPS: 'Orange Cutie' requires 100 days from seed. To plant, sow seeds 1 inch deep directly into garden when the soil temperature reaches 65°F and no frost threatens. Space the plants 3 to 4 feet apart or plant one vine per 5-gallon container.

CARE REQUIREMENTS: Good pollination is essential for pumpkin production. Like other varieties, the male flowers open first and have straight stems, while female flowers open later and have a mini-pumpkin at their base. Plant plenty of flowers near the vines to ensure lots of pollinators are around. Provide plants with consistent moisture, and leave the fruits on the vine until they're fully colored.

HARVEST TIME: Fall

Astia Zucchini

COMMON NAME: Astia Zucchini

BOTANICAL NAME: *Cucurbita pepo* 'Astia'

MATURE DIMENSIONS: 18 inches tall; 2 to 2½ feet wide

PHYSICAL APPEARANCE: A favorite zucchini of container gardeners, 'Astia's' deep, glossy green fruits are best picked when 6 to 7 inches long. The plants are only half the width of other varieties, and their open habit makes harvesting a snap. 'Astia' is resistant to powdery mildew and produces very early (just 38 to 42 days after planting!).

PLANTING TIPS: This compact, hybrid zucchini is best started by sowing the seeds directly into the garden or container when the threat of frost has passed and summer weather has arrived. Plant the seeds 1 inch deep and 3 feet apart, or plant one plant per 5- to 8-gallon container.

CARE REQUIREMENTS: As with other squash, good pollination is key for ample fruit set. If your zucchini have misshapen ends or fail to grow, it's a sure sign of poor pollination. Plant this variety alongside flowers to increase the number of pollinating insects present. Harvest by cutting the fruits from the vine; do not pull. Harvest on a daily basis to ensure continual zucchini production.

HARVEST TIME: Summer through fall

Patio Star Zucchini

COMMON NAME: Patio Star Zucchini

BOTANICAL NAME: *Cucurbita pepo* 'Patio Star'

MATURE DIMENSIONS: 18 inches tall; 2 feet wide

PHYSICAL APPEARANCE: A patio-perfect zucchini if there ever was one! The dark green, shiny fruit is thin skinned and flavorful. With green leaves edged in white and a prolific production rate, 'Patio Star' is indeed a star of the patio. Plants mature in 50 days from seed. This hybrid is half the size of standard plants.

PLANTING TIPS: To plant, sow the seeds directly into the garden 1 inch deep and 3 feet apart or plant one plant per 5- to 8-gallon container. Since zucchini plants are frost sensitive, wait to plant until frost no longer threatens. For continuous harvests, sow a few new seeds every few weeks.

CARE REQUIREMENTS: For the best production, keep the soil evenly moist throughout the plant's growth cycle. Harvest by cutting the fruit from vine; do not pull. If you have poor fruit set or the zucchinis are misshapen, poor pollination may be a factor.

HARVEST TIME: Summer through fall

Honey Bear Winter Squash

COMMON NAME: Honey Bear Winter Squash

BOTANICAL NAME: *Cucurbita pepo* 'Honey Bear'

MATURE DIMENSIONS: 2 feet tall; 4 feet wide

PHYSICAL APPEARANCE: This gorgeous hybrid acorn squash has a rind that's deep green and flesh that's rich orange. Each fruit weighs 1 to 1¼ pounds. The compact bush plants do not vine and take over the garden, and they're resistant to powdery mildew. Expect each plant to produce three to four fruits. At half the size of a standard variety, this heavy-yielding winter squash is a true award winner.

PLANTING TIPS: It's best to wait until after the danger of frost has passed to sow seeds directly in the garden. You can also start seeds indoors under grow lights about 4 weeks prior to your last frost date, if you live where the growing season is short. When starting plants indoors, try not to disturb the roots when transplanting them out into the garden. Seeds should be sown 1 inch deep and spaced 3 feet apart, or plant one plant per 8- to 10-gallon container. 'Honey Bear' requires 100 days from seed to reach maturity

CARE REQUIREMENTS: Mulch winter squash with several inches of straw or shredded leaves to retain soil moisture and limit weeds. Allow the fruits to ripen on the vine until a yellow spot appears on the bottom side of the fruit where it touches the soil, about 55 days after the plants come into flower.

HARVEST TIME: Late summer through fall

Sugarbush Winter Squash

COMMON NAME: Sugarbush Winter Squash

BOTANICAL NAME: *Cucurbita pepo* 'Sugarbush'

MATURE DIMENSIONS: 2 feet tall; 4 to 5 feet wide

PHYSICAL APPEARANCE: 'Sugarbush' is an acorn-type winter squash with dark-skinned fruits and deep orange flesh. The compact, bushy plants are resistant to powdery mildew and ready to harvest about 90 days after planting. The 2½-pound fruits are sweet with an excellent texture.

PLANTING TIPS: If you live where the growing season is short, plant seeds indoors under grow lights about 4 weeks before your last expected spring frost. Move the plants outdoors when the weather warms. If you live where summers are long and warm, sow the seeds directly into the garden after the threat of frost has passed. Plant seeds 1 inch deep and 3 feet apart, or plant one plant per 8 to 10 gallon container.

CARE REQUIREMENTS: Harvest the squash when their rinds are hard and they have an orange patch on the bottom where they touch the ground. Leave a short stem on the squash when cutting them from the vine.

HARVEST TIME: Late summer through fall

Totem Tomato

COMMON NAME: Totem Tomato

BOTANICAL NAME: *Solanum lycopersicum* 'Totem'

MATURE DIMENSIONS: 18 to 30 inches tall; 18 inches wide

PHYSICAL APPEARANCE: A compact and highly productive tomato, 'Totem' is ready to harvest just 70 days from transplant. It bears tons of 1- to 2-inch, bright red fruit in large clusters on beefy little plants. The foliage is lush and beautiful, making this variety great for front porch pots and deck planters.

PLANTING TIPS: Sow the seeds indoors under grow lights about 6 weeks before the average last frost date. Then, transplant the seedlings outside after the danger of frost has passed. Like other tomatoes, bury the plants deeply to encourage the development of an extensive root system. Space plants 3 feet apart, or put one plant per 3- to 5-gallon pot.

CARE REQUIREMENTS: Provide consistent moisture to avoid blossom end rot, especially when growing 'Totem' in a container. Mulching the plants helps keep the soil evenly moist, too. The short and stocky growth habit of this variety means no staking is required.

HARVEST TIME: Summer through fall

Super Bush Tomato

COMMON NAME: Super Bush Tomato

BOTANICAL NAME: *Solanum lycopersicum* 'Super Bush'

MATURE DIMENSIONS: 2 to 3 feet tall; 1 to 2 feet wide

PHYSICAL APPEARANCE: These saladette tomatoes weigh in at 5 to 6 ounces each and fit nicely in the palm of your hand. Their sweet flavor is ready to enjoy about 70 days after the transplants are settled into the garden. A hybrid variety with high yields, the dark green foliage is very attractive.

PLANTING TIPS: Sow seeds of 'Super Bush' indoors under grow lights about 6 weeks before the last expected spring frost. Move the seedlings into the garden when frost no longer threatens. Space the plants 3 to 4 feet apart, or put one plant per 5- to 8-gallon container. Bury the plants deeply to encourage good root growth, and mulch well with straw or shredded leaves to optimize the soil's moisture retention.

CARE REQUIREMENTS: Due to the heavy production of this plant, use a tomato cage or staking system to keep the vines upright. Regularly prune excessive leaf growth to encourage tomato production.

HARVEST TIME: Summer through fall

Bush Goliath Tomato

COMMON NAME: Bush Goliath Tomato

BOTANICAL NAME: *Solanum lycopersicum* 'Bush Goliath'

MATURE DIMENSIONS: 3 feet tall; 1½ feet wide

PHYSICAL APPEARANCE: This variety is always a surprise! Good-sized, 6- to 8-ounce fruits measure 3 to 4 inches wide and are incredibly prolific. Their bright red coloration is perfectly consistent, and the flavor is delish! Ready to pick 68 days from transplant, these determined vines produce clusters of fruit all summer long.

PLANTING TIPS: Sow seeds indoors under grow lights 6 weeks before moving the transplants outdoors. Bury the stems deeply when planting, allowing just the top few leaves to stick above the soil line. If you're growing 'Bush Goliath' in a pot, one that's between 8 and 10 gallons is ideal. Or, space the plants 3 to 4 feet apart in the garden.

CARE REQUIREMENTS: Keep the soil consistently moist to avoid blossom end rot. Mulch the plants with 2 to 3 inches of straw or shredded leaves. Provide a tomato cage or stake to support the fruit-laden stems, especially as the season progresses.

HARVEST TIME: Summer through fall

Red Profusion Tomato

COMMON NAME: Red Profusion Tomato

BOTANICAL NAME: *Solanum lycopersicum* 'Red Profusion'

MATURE DIMENSIONS: 6 inches tall; 2 feet wide

PHYSICAL APPEARANCE: 'Red Profusion' is an exceptional choice for pots and hanging baskets. The trailing vines of this hybrid form a mound and produce fruits that are 1 inch across, deep red, and intensely flavorful. The highly branched growth habit of this selection looks great tumbling over the edge of a raised planter or garden container.

PLANTING TIPS: These compact plants are best for containers due to their sprawling growth habit. Fast production (just 47 days after transplanting!) means you'll have an early and prolific harvest. Start the seeds indoors under grow lights 6 weeks before the danger of frost passes. Plant one transplant per large hanging basket or 2- to 3-gallon pot.

CARE REQUIREMENTS: Ensure each plant receives consistent and regular irrigation. Containerized tomatoes are prone to blossom end rot and keeping them properly watered prevents this disorder. Harvest ripe tomatoes on a continual basis to encourage more blooms and subsequent fruits.

HARVEST TIME: Summer through fall

Tumbling Tom Tomato

COMMON NAME: Tumbling Tom Tomato

BOTANICAL NAME: *Solanum lycopersicum*
'Tumbling Tom'

MATURE DIMENSIONS: 6 to 8 inches tall;
12 inches wide

PHYSICAL APPEARANCE: The short, cascading vines of 'Tumbling Tom' make this variety the quintessential choice for containers of all types. Red or yellow cherry-type tomatoes are produced prolifically 65 to 70 days after transplant. These little cuties look so pretty in window boxes, hanging baskets, and vertical gardens of any shape and size.

PLANTING TIPS: Sow seeds of 'Tumbling Tom' indoors under grow lights 6 weeks before the danger of frost passes. In spring, when frost no longer threatens, plant the transplants outdoors by sinking their stems deeply into the ground. This encourages good root production on all types of tomatoes. Plant one vine per 2- to 3-gallon container.

CARE REQUIREMENTS: There's no need to stake 'Tumbling Tom' plants due to their rambling growth habit, but it's best to grow this selection in a pot and not in the ground. Pick the tomatoes as soon as they're ripe to encourage further production. Water regularly and give the plants maximum sunlight.

HARVEST TIME: Summer through fall

Sugar Pot Watermelon

COMMON NAME: Sugar Pot Watermelon

BOTANICAL NAME: *Citrullus lanatus* 'Sugar Pot'

MATURE DIMENSIONS: 1 foot tall; 2 to 3 feet wide

PHYSICAL APPEARANCE: Patio- and small-garden friendly, this compact watermelon variety won't take up a lot of real estate. Each plant produces two or three 5- to 8-pound fruits. 'Sugar Pot' is a hybrid variety with melons that are juicy and red fleshed. Its leaves are smaller than most other watermelon varieties, too.

PLANTING TIPS: Sow seeds directly into the garden several weeks after the danger of frost has passed and the soil temperature is about 80°F. Watermelons resent transplanting, so if you do start seeds indoors to get a jump on the growing season, use plantable peat pots and don't disturb the roots when transplanting. Space the plants 5 feet apart or grow one vine per 5-gallon pot.

CARE REQUIREMENTS: Consistent moisture is key to good fruit production. The melons will crack if a dry spell is followed by excessive moisture. To ensure good pollination, plant near flowers.

HARVEST TIME: Summer

Spicy Globe Basil

COMMON NAME: Spicy Globe Basil

BOTANICAL NAME: *Ocimum basilicum* 'Spicy Globe'

MATURE DIMENSIONS: 1 foot tall; 1 foot wide

PHYSICAL APPEARANCE: A true herbal delight, 'Spicy Globe' basil offers a classic basil taste with a bit of a spicy bite. The globe-shaped plants are covered in dense branches of small, very aromatic leaves. The flowers are tiny and white and should be pinched off for the best foliage flavor. 'Spicy Globe' is a petite and uniform plant that makes a lovely edge for garden beds.

PLANTING TIPS: Purchase starter plants from a nursery or sow seeds indoors under grow lights 6 weeks before the last expected spring frost. Move the plants outdoors only when there's no remaining threat of frost. The dense, compact growth habit of this variety means you can space them fairly close; 18 inches apart on center. Or, plant in mixed containers, hanging baskets, window boxes, or raised beds.

CARE REQUIREMENTS: Basil is not frost tolerant, so protect it from cold temperatures. Pinch the plants back regularly or harvest frequently for continuous production of new foliage.

HARVEST TIME: Early summer through frost

Fino Verde Basil

COMMON NAME: Fino Verde Basil

BOTANICAL NAME: *Ocimum basilicum* 'Fino Verde'

MATURE DIMENSIONS: 10 to 12 inches tall; equal spread

PHYSICAL APPEARANCE: 'Fino Verde' is a compact, bushy basil that's covered in flavorful, tiny leaves. It flowers much later than full-sized varieties, so you don't have to pinch it back as frequently. With thick growth and a dense branching habit, 'Fino Verde' is both tidy and productive.

PLANTING TIPS: Purchase starter plants from a nursery, or sow seeds indoors under grow lights 6 weeks before the last expected spring frost. Space plants 18 inches on center, or grow one plant per 1-gallon container.

CARE REQUIREMENTS: This fast-growing variety requires very little care. Simply pinch off flowers as they're produced and make regular harvests to encourage new, succulent growth. With this variety's classic sweet basil taste, you can't go wrong!

HARVEST TIME: Early summer through frost

Everleaf Basil

COMMON NAME: Everleaf Basil

BOTANICAL NAME: *Ocimum basilicum* 'Everleaf'

MATURE DIMENSIONS: 18 inches tall; 12 inches wide

PHYSICAL APPEARANCE: This variety boasts full-sized basil leaves on a compact plant! Very productive and decently resistant to downy mildew, 'Everleaf' bolts an average of 8 weeks later than standard sweet basil. That means very little pinching is required and the harvest is prolonged. Each leaf is 2 to 3 inches long with a classic sweet basil scent and flavor. Short stems between leaf nodes keep this variety compact.

PLANTING TIPS: Purchase transplants from a nursery, or sow seeds indoors under grow lights 6 weeks before the last expected spring frost. Basil is frost sensitive, so wait to move the plants outdoors until nights are consistently warm. Space plants 18 inches apart, or put one plant per 2-gallon container.

CARE REQUIREMENTS: Regular harvests generate new leaves; pick as often as you'd like. Pinch off flowers when they arrive for the best foliage flavor. Good air circulation is critical when growing basil.

HARVEST TIME: Early summer through frost

Elfin Thyme

COMMON NAME: Elfin Thyme

BOTANICAL NAME: *Thymus serphyllum* 'Elfin'

MATURE DIMENSIONS: 1 to 2 inches tall; 12 to 18 inches wide

PHYSICAL APPEARANCE: This low-growing, tough perennial herb is not only good in the kitchen, it's also good for pollinators. Lavender-pink flowers appear in early summer above tiny leaves with a classic thyme flavor.

PLANTING TIPS: 'Elfin' thyme can be started from seed sown indoors under grow lights about 10 weeks before the start of the gardening season, but it's probably best to purchase starter plants from a nursery. The plants form a dense groundcover when spaced closely. Or, plant it in a mixed herb container, raised bed, or a small herb garden.

CARE REQUIREMENTS: Thyme is a very low-maintenance, drought-tolerant, tough plant that's winter hardy down to −30°F. Trim back dead growth in the early spring and harvest the leaves as needed.

HARVEST TIME: Spring through fall

Sweet Marjoram

COMMON NAME: Sweet Marjoram

BOTANICAL NAME: *Origanum majorana*

MATURE DIMENSIONS: 12 to 18 inches tall; equal spread

PHYSICAL APPEARANCE: This naturally low-growing herb looks great as an edging, groundcover, or when planted in pots. The green leaves and knob-like clusters of white to pink flowers have a sprawling habit and a delicious flavor. Enjoyed fresh or dried, sweet marjoram is very versatile in the kitchen.

PLANTING TIPS: Start from seed sown indoors in late winter, or purchase starter plants from the nursery. A fairly slow-growing herb, sweet marjoram is not tolerant of frosts, so wait until warm temperatures arrive before planting outdoors.

CARE REQUIREMENTS: For maximum production, make continual harvests of the leaves and stems. Trim off the flowers for the best leaf production and flavor. At the end of the growing season, marjoram plants can be overwintered indoors on a sunny windowsill.

HARVEST TIME: Midsummer through frost

Fine Leaf Chives

COMMON NAME: Fine Leaf Chives

BOTANICAL NAME: *Allium schoenoprasum* 'Fine Leaf'

MATURE DIMENSIONS: 12 inches tall; 10 inches wide

PHYSICAL APPEARANCE: The grass-like, slender, onion-flavored leaves of 'Fine Leaf' chives stay tender even when mature. Balls of pink to purple, edible flowers occur in the spring. The vase shape of this plant looks great in a garden border, container, or small herb garden.

PLANTING TIPS: Sow seeds directly into the garden ¼ inch deep and 2 inches apart. Thin the resulting seedlings to 10 inches apart. It may be best, however, to purchase a starter plant from a nursery as most households really need only one or two plants. Chives are a perennial herb that's winter hardy down to −40°F.

CARE REQUIREMENTS: Enjoy the fresh leaves throughout the growing season by cutting them off at their base. After flowering, cut the entire plant back to the ground to generate tender new growth.

HARVEST TIME: Spring to fall

Wega Parsley

COMMON NAME: Wega Parsley

BOTANICAL NAME: *Petroselinum crispum* 'Wega'

MATURE DIMENSIONS: 10 to 12 inches; equal spread

PHYSICAL APPEARANCE: The upright growth habit of 'Wega' means it takes up less garden space than most other varieties. This curly leaved parsley variety produces dark green, classic parsley leaves with a clean taste and crisp texture. 'Wega' doesn't turn bitter in the heat.

PLANTING TIPS: Sow seeds indoors under grow lights about 8 weeks before the last expected spring frost date. It may take 3 to 4 weeks for the seeds to germinate. Move the plants into the garden or outdoor containers at the start of the growing season. Space plants 1 foot apart.

CARE REQUIREMENTS: Well-drained soil is a must when growing parsley. Harvest the leaves regularly for continued production. Parsley is a cold-tolerant biennial herb that will overwinter in mild climates and flower at the start of its second season. After flowering, replace the plants with fresh stock for the best flavor.

HARVEST TIME: Spring through fall in the north; fall through spring in the south

SOURCE LIST

Note: As you browse this list of plant sources, be aware that those marked as wholesalers do not sell direct to the consumer. However, many of these companies have a "Search for a Retailer" feature on their websites so that you can find a local nursery or garden center near you that carries their plants.

American Beauties Native Plants (wholesale)
1170 Old Lancaster Pike
Hockessin, DE 19707
USA
www.abnativeplants.com

American Meadows
2438 Shelburne Rd., Suite 1
Shelburne, VT 05482
USA
877-309-7333
www.americanmeadows.com

Arrowhead Alpines
1310 North Gregory Rd.
PO Box 857
Fowlerville, MI 48836
USA
517-223-3581
www.arrowheadalpines.com

Bailey Nurseries (wholesale)
1325 Bailey Rd.
St. Paul, MN 55119
USA
800-829-8898
www.baileynurseries.com

Baker Creek Heirloom Seeds
2278 Baker Creek Rd.
Mansfield, MO 65704
USA
417-924-8917
www.rareseeds.com

Ball Seed
622 Town Rd.
West Chicago, IL 60185
USA
800-879-BALL
www.ballseed.com

Bloomin' Easy (wholesale)
34825 Hallert Rd.
Abbotsford, BC V3G 1R3
Canada
www.bloomineasyplants.com

Bluestone Perennials
7211 Middle Ridge Rd.
Madison, OH 44057
USA
800-852-5243
www.bluestoneperennials.com

Bonnie Plants (wholesale)
1727 Highway 223
Union Springs, AL 36089
USA
www.bonnieplants.com

Broken Arrow Nursery
13 Broken Arrow Rd.
Hamden, CT 06518
USA
203-288-1026
www.brokenarrownursery.com

Burpee Seed Company
300 Park Ave.
Warminster, PA 18974
USA
800-888-1447
www.burpee.com

Bushel and Berry
800-457-1859
www.bushelandberry.com

Conifer Kingdom
6450 Brush Creek Dr. NE
Silverton, OR 97381
USA
503-874-4123
www.coniferkingdom.com

The Crape Myrtle Company
352-486-5722
www.crapemyrtles.com

Easy Elegance Roses
(wholesale)
www.easyeleganceroses.com

First Editions Plants
(wholesale)
www.firsteditionsplants.com

Garden Debut (wholesale)
28406 Highway 82
Park Hill, OK 74451
USA
877-663-5053
www.gardendebut.com

Gardener's Confidence Collection (wholesale)
www.gardenersconfidence.com

Greenleaf Nursery Company
(wholesale)
2349 Chinquapin Rd.
Tarboro, NC 27886
USA
877-331-2982
www.greenleafnursery.com

Heritage Seedlings (wholesale)
71st Ave. SE
Salem, OR 97317
USA
503-585-9835
www.heritageseedlings.com

High Country Gardens
2438 Shelburne Rd., Suite 1
Shelburne, VT 05482
USA
800-925-9387
www.highcountrygardens.com

High Mowing Organic Seeds
76 Quarry Rd.
Wolcott, VT 05680
USA
866-735-4454
www.highmowingseeds.com

Iseli Nursery (wholesale)
www.iselinursery.com

J. Frank Schmidt & Son Co.
(wholesale)
9500 SE 327th Ave.
Boring, OR 97009
USA
503-663-2121
www.jfschmidt.com

J. W. Jung Seed Company
335 S. High St.
Randolph, WI 53956
USA
800-247-5864
www.jungseed.com

Jackson & Perkins
800-292-4769
www.jacksonandperkins.com

Johnny's Selected Seeds
PO Box 299
Waterville, ME 04903
USA
877-564-6697
www.johnnyseeds.com

Kigi Nursery
121 Noble Ridge Dr.
Kelso, WA 98626
USA
www.kiginursery.com

**Klehm's Song Sparrow Farm
and Nursery**
13101 E. Rye Rd.
Avalon, WI 53505
USA
608-883-2356
www.songsparrow.com

Klyn Nurseries (wholesale)
3322 S. Ridge Rd.
PO Box 343
Perry, OH 44081
USA
www.klynnurseries.com
800-860-8104

Lake Valley Seed
5717 Arapahoe Ave.
Boulder, CO 80303
USA
800-333-4882
www.lakevalleyseed.com

McKay Nursery Company
PO Box 185
750 S. Monroe St.
Waterloo, WI 53594
USA
920-478-2121
www.mckaynursery.com

Midwest Groundcovers
PO Box 748
St. Charles, IL 60174
USA
847-742-1790
www.midwestgroundcovers.com

Monrovia
817 E. Monrovia Pl.
Azusa, CA 91702
USA
www.monrovia.com

Nature Hills Nursery
9910 N. 48th St., Suite 200
Omaha, NE 68152
USA
888-864-7663
www.naturehills.com

New Life Nursery & Garden
314 Highway 8 E
Pelzer, SC 29669
USA
www.newlifenursery1.net

New Moon Nursery (wholesale)
975 Barretts Run Rd.
Bridgeton, NJ 08302
USA
888-998-1951
www.newmoonnursery.com

North Creek Nurseries
(wholesale)
388 N. Creek Rd.
Landenberg, PA 19350
USA
877-ECO-PLUG
www.northcreeknurseries.com

Park Seed
800-845-3369
www.parkseed.com

**Planting Tree Online
Garden Center**
241 Mazeppa Rd.
Mooresville, NC 28115
USA
855-541-7526
www.plantingtree.com

Plants Nouveau
PO Box 40125
Mobile, AL 36640
USA
www.plantsnouveau.com

Pleasant Run Nursery
(wholesale)
PO Box 247
Allentown, NJ 08501
USA
609-259-8585
www.pleasantrunnursery.com

Proven Winners (wholesale)
111 E. Elm St., Suite D
Sycamore, IL 60178
USA
815-895-8130
www.provenwinners.com

Reimer Seeds
PO Box 206
Saint Leonard, MD 20685
USA
www.reimerseeds.com

Renee's Garden
6060 Graham Hill Rd.
Felton, CA 95018
USA
888-880-7228
www.reneesgarden.com

Russell's Nursery (wholesale)
24766 NE Airport Rd.
Aurora, OR 97002
USA
503-678-2536
www.russellsnursery.com

Seed Savers Exchange
3094 N. Winn Rd.
Decora, IA 52101
USA
563-382-5990
www.seedsavers.org

Sooner Plant Farm
25976 S. 524 Rd.
Park Hill, OK 74451
USA
918-453-0771
www.soonerplantfarm.com

Spring Meadow Nursery
(wholesale)
12601 120th Ave.
Grand Haven, MI 49417
USA
800-633-8859
www.springmeadownursery.com

Star Roses & Plants (wholesale)
800-457-1859
www.starrosesandplants.com

Terra Nova Nurseries
(wholesale)
10051 S. Macksburg Rd.
Canby, OR 97013
USA
800-215-9450
www.terranovanurseries.com

Territorial Seed Company
PO Box 158
Cottage Grove, OR 97424
USA
800-626-0866
www.territorialseed.com

Totally Tomatoes
800-345-5977
www.totallytomato.com

Van Belle Nursery (wholesale)
34825 Hallert Rd.
Abbotsford, BC V3G 1R3
Canada
888-826-2355
www.vanbelle.com

Victory Seed Company
PO Box 192
Molalla, OR 97038
USA
503-829-3126
www.victoryseeds.com

Walters Gardens (wholesale)
1992 96th Ave.
Zeeland, MI
USA
800-WALTERS
www.waltersgardens.com

Wayside Gardens
800-845-1124
www.waysidegardens.com

White Flower Farm
PO Box 50, Route 63
Litchfield, CT 06759
USA
800-503-9624
www.whiteflowerfarm.com

ADDITIONAL RESOURCES

Garden-pedia by Pamela Bennett and Maria Zampini

The Less Is More Garden: Big Ideas for Designing Your Small Yard by Susan Morrison

Dirr's Hardy Trees and Shrubs by Michael Dirr

Dirr's Encyclopedia of Trees & Shrubs by Michael Dirr

Manual of Woody Landscape Plants by Michael and Bonnie Dirr

Taylor's Guide to Shrubs by Kathleen Fisher

New Small Garden: Contemporary Principles, Planting and Practice by Noel Kingsbury and Maayke de Ridder

Big Dreams, Small Garden: A Guide to Creating Something Extraordinary in Your Ordinary Space by Marianne Willburn

Royal Horticultural Society Small Garden Handbook: Making the Most of Your Outdoor Space by Andrew Wilson

Small-Space Vegetable Gardens: Growing Great Edibles in Containers, Raised Beds, and Small Plots by Andrea Bellamy

Container Gardening Complete: Creative Projects for Growing Vegetables and Flowers in Small Spaces by Jessica Walliser

Small Space Garden Ideas by Philippa Pearson

ABOUT THE AUTHOR

Horticulturist Jessica Walliser cohosts *The Organic Gardeners*, an award–winning program on KDKA Radio in Pittsburgh, Pennsylvania. She is a former contributing editor for *Organic Gardening* magazine and a regular contributor to many regional and national magazines, including *Fine Gardening* and *Hobby Farms*.

Her two weekly gardening columns for the *Pittsburgh Tribune-Review* have been enjoyed by readers for over 10 years. Jessica's fourth book, *Attracting Beneficial Bugs to the Garden: A Natural Approach to Pest Control*, was awarded the American Horticultural Society's 2014 Book Award.

Jessica received her degree in ornamental horticulture from The Pennsylvania State University. She's taught a diverse array of gardening topics for over 20 years and was awarded the 2018 Gold Award for a Live Presentation from the Association for Garden Communicators.

Jessica cofounded the gardening website SavvyGardening.com to cultivate curiosity and confidence in gardeners by providing them with innovative ideas, tips, and advice.

Follow Jessica and her gardening adventures at

WEBSITES: www.jessicawalliser.com and www.savvygardening.com

FACEBOOK: Jessica Walliser (www.facebook.com/jessica.walliser)

TWITTER: @jessicawalliser (www.twitter.com/jessicawalliser)

INSTAGRAM: @jessicawalliser

PINTEREST: Savvy Gardening (www.pinterest.com/savvygardening)

BLOG: Savvy Gardening (www.savvygardening.com)

PHOTO CREDITS

ABZ Seeds 148;

Bailey Nurseries, Inc. 110, 111; **Baker Creek Heirloom Seeds / Rareseeds.com** 89, 89, 149, 167, 170; **Ball Horticultural Company** 80 (middle right), 89 (top right), 135, 138, 163; **Bloomin' Easy®** 86 (top right), 102; **Bluestone Perennials** 86 (top left), 92 (top left), 92 (top right), 130; **Bonnie Plants** 166, 184; **botanikfoto. com** 123; **Bushel and Berry** 144, 145, 146, 147;

Concept Plants BV 139; **Conifer Kingdom / Sam Pratt** 16, 92 (bottom left), 95 (bottom center); **Cultivaris GmbH** 137;

Dave Wilson Nursery 151, 152;

Eva Monheim 116;

First Edition Plants 99 (middle right[b]), 115;

Garden Center Marketing 125; **Garden Debut** (Greenleaf Nursery Company) 150; **Gardener's Confidence Collection** 113;

High Country Gardens 83 (top right), 89 (middle center), 136; **High Mowing Seeds** 176, 181;

Iseli Nursery / Randall C. Smith Photographer 83 (middle center), 92 (bottom center), 92 (bottom right), 95 (middle), 95 (bottom left), 95 (bottom right);

J. Frank Schmidt & Son Co. 83 (top left), 83 (middle right), 118, 118, 121, 122; **Janet Loughrey with design by Helena Wagner, 4 Season Gardens, 4seasongardens.com** 8, 12, 48; **Jessica Walliser** 11, 14, 17, 18, 19, 20, 22, 23, 24, 28, 29, 31, 32, 34, 36, 40, 41, 43, 44, 45, 46, 47, 47, 49, 50, 53, 74, 99 (top right), 142, 157, 160, 172, 179, 187, 188, 195, 200; **Johnny's Selected Seeds / Kristen Earley** 159, 165, 180, 190, 193, 194; **www. songsparrow.com** 119;

Klyn Nursery 83 (middle left);

MilletteGardenPictures.com 77 (middle right), 77 (bottom left), 77 (bottom right), 83 (bottom left), 89 (middle left [t]), 95 (top right), 99 (bottom right), 112, 117, 124, 126, 191; **Missouri Botanical Garden** 89 (middle left [b]);

Niki Jabbour 114, 189; **North Creek Nurseries** 77 (top right), 83 (bottom right), 86 (bottom right), 92 (top center), 99 (middle left), 129;

Plant Haven 100, 120; **Plants Nouveau** 77 (bottom center), 92 (middle center), 99 (top left), 108, 141; **Pleasant Run Nursery** 77 (middle left), 95 (top left); **Plug Connection** 153; **Proven Winners (www. provenwinners.com)** 77 (top left), 80 (top left), 80 (top right), 80 (bottom left), 86 (middle right), 86 (bottom left), 89 (top left), 89 (middle right), 99 (middle right[t]), 103, 104, 105, 106, 107;

reneesgarden.com 155, 158, 162, 168, 169, 171, 175, 178, 183; **Rutgers University Pat Bzdek (NJ)** 89 (bottom left);

Shutterstock.com 25, 26, 38, 42, 161; **Siegers Seed Company** 177; **Star® Roses and Plants** 80 (bottom right);

TERRA NOVA 128; **Tesselaar Plants** 133; **Totally Tomatoes** 174, 182; **Vegetalis** 185, 186;

W. Atlee Burpee Company 154, 156, 161, 164, 173, 192; **Walters Gardens, Inc.** 80 (top right), 86 (top center), 86 (middle left), 89 (bottom right), 92 (middle right), 99 (bottom left), 127, 131, 132, 134, 140.

METRIC CONVERSIONS

Metric Equivalent

Inches (in.)	1/64	1/32	1/25	1/16	1/8	1/4	3/8	2/5	1/2	5/8	3/4	7/8	1	2	3	4	5	6	7	8	9	10	11	12	36	39.4
Feet (ft.)																								1	3	3 1/12
Yards (yd.)																									1	1 1/12
Millimeters (mm)	0.40	0.79	1	1.59	3.18	6.35	9.53	10	12.7	15.9	19.1	22.2	25.4	50.8	76.2	101.6	127	152	178	203	229	254	279	305	914	1,000
Centimeters (cm)							0.95	1	1.27	1.59	1.91	2.22	2.54	5.08	7.62	10.16	12.7	15.2	17.8	20.3	22.9	25.4	27.9	30.5	91.4	100
Meters (m)																								.30	.91	1.00

Converting Measurements

TO CONVERT:	TO:	MULTIPLY BY:
Inches	Millimeters	25.4
Inches	Centimeters	2.54
Feet	Meters	0.305
Yards	Meters	0.914
Miles	Kilometers	1.609
Square inches	Square centimeters	6.45
Square feet	Square meters	0.093
Square yards	Square meters	0.836
Cubic inches	Cubic centimeters	16.4
Cubic feet	Cubic meters	0.0283
Cubic yards	Cubic meters	0.765
Pints (U.S.)	Liters	0.473 (Imp. 0.568)
Quarts (U.S.)	Liters	0.946 (Imp. 1.136)
Gallons (U.S.)	Liters	3.785 (Imp. 4.546)
Ounces	Grams	28.4
Pounds	Kilograms	0.454
Tons	Metric tons	0.907

TO CONVERT:	TO:	MULTIPLY BY:
Millimeters	Inches	0.039
Centimeters	Inches	0.394
Meters	Feet	3.28
Meters	Yards	1.09
Kilometers	Miles	0.621
Square centimeters	Square inches	0.155
Square meters	Square feet	10.8
Square meters	Square yards	1.2
Cubic centimeters	Cubic inches	0.061
Cubic meters	Cubic feet	35.3
Cubic meters	Cubic yards	1.31
Liters	Pints (U.S.)	2.114 (Imp. 1.76)
Liters	Quarts (U.S.)	1.057 (Imp. 0.88)
Liters	Gallons (U.S.)	0.264 (Imp. 0.22)
Grams	Ounces	0.035
Kilograms	Pounds	2.2
Metric tons	Tons	1.1

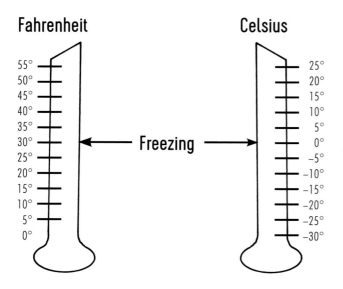

Fahrenheit — Celsius thermometer scales, with "Freezing" marked between 30°F and 0°C.

Converting Temperatures

Convert degrees Fahrenheit (F) to degrees Celsius (C) by following this simple formula: Subtract 32 from the Fahrenheit temperature reading. Then multiply that number by 5/9. For example, 77°F - 32 = 45. 45 × 5/9 = 25°C.

To convert degrees Celsius to degrees Fahrenheit, multiply the Celsius temperature reading by 9/5, then add 32. For example, 25°C × 9/5 = 45. 45 + 32 = 77°F.

INDEX